THE 2-HOUR COCKTAIL PARTY

THE 2-HOUR COCKTAIL PARTY

HOW TO BUILD BIG RELATIONSHIPS WITH SMALL GATHERINGS

NICK GRAY

LIONCREST
PUBLISHING

THE 2-HOUR COCKTAIL PARTY
How to Build Big Relationships with Small Gatherings

ISBN   978-1-5445-3007-9   *Paperback*
           978-1-5445-3006-2   *Ebook*
           978-1-5445-2915-8   *Audiobook*

Contents

PART 3
Party Time

APPENDICES

Introduction

Tyler Vawser moved to Little Rock, Arkansas so his wife could be closer to her family.

Tyler had no job and no connections when they got there. He didn't know a single person in town except for his wife's family. He felt alone and worried about his career. He didn't even have a friend he could text on a Friday night.

Today, Tyler's life is completely different. He hosts popular gatherings that have a long waiting list of interesting people. He's become a vice president in charge of hiring for a major education company. His life feels full, he makes more money, and he has new friends and colleagues that inspire him.

What changed? He started to host small parties. Tyler created new connections and built up his relationships using the instructions in this book. I'll finish his story in Chapter 5— it's a good one.

You'll meet other first-time hosts in special "Party People Profiles" throughout this book. Like Tyler, they all wanted something more in life—but they never considered hosting a party could make that happen.

Thanks to my unique cocktail party formula, which in turn helped them build new relationships, they dramatically enriched and transformed their lives. All from spending seven dollars on a pack of name tags and one hundred dollars on various drinks and snacks.

This book worked for them, and it will work for you.

Hi, My Name is Nick Gray

I've created a lot of fantastic, meaningful relationships in my life. I count business owners, engineers, teachers, artists, and many interesting people who are just fun to hang out with as my friends.

I get to spend quality time with many of them—usually every single week.

Those friends helped me turn my wacky weekend hobby, Museum Hack, into a full-fledged business that gives "renegade tours" at the Metropolitan Museum of Art. I never thought this would happen, but that side hustle grew into a multimillion-dollar company.

Before I sold Museum Hack in 2019, we had fifty employees and were working in some of the biggest museums in the world, like the Art Institute of Chicago and the Getty Museum in Los Angeles. My company was included in the Inc. 5000 as one of the fastest growing privately held businesses in America. I gave a popular TEDx talk and was featured multiple times in the *Washington Post, New York Times, Wall Street Journal,* and other major media outlets.[1]

When I moved to New York City in 2007, I only knew a few people. I was a socially awkward twenty-something from a middle-class background trying to make it in the big city.

In social situations, I sometimes felt overwhelmed and intimidated. My heart would race, and I'd stutter or say something embarrassing. Entering a room full of strangers was scary. If I got invited to a party, I would hang by the bar and play with my phone. In my braver moments, I'd hover on the sidelines waiting for the perfect moment to join a conversation.

---

1 For links to these articles and to see my TEDx Talk, visit www.party.pro/mypress.

That moment never came. Instead, I'd find a reason to leave the party early and go home alone. I felt sad and low, like I'd wasted my time. I always took it personally. It frustrated me that a city of millions of people could make me feel so lonely.

You might be wondering how I went from there to where I am now: how did I go from sitting home alone on Friday nights to having a packed calendar and lots of meaningful relationships?

Well, as you'll see in this book, the solution was simple...

Don't Attend Bad Events— Host Great Parties Instead

Instead of going to random bars or meetups to try to create new connections, I decided to go a different route. Instead of going to other peoples' parties, I decided to bring the party to me.

What I discovered, through lots of trial and error, is that there's a specific way to structure parties to make them easy and successful—a "formula," if you will, that anyone can follow.

Over the last ten years, I've hosted hundreds of these small parties. Then I've spent the past few years writing this book and testing every single aspect of it with different people around the world.

What follows in these pages is my formula to "hack" your social life by learning how to throw parties. I'll show you how to easily host fun events in your own home. You'll become very good at hosting a gathering, just as I have helped tens of thousands of people to appreciate the art inside the Met.

Some people may think a party requires loud music, late nights, and tons of booze. But a party is simply where people get together and have a good time. There can be an explicit purpose such as playing board games, celebrating an event, or meeting new people. But the essence of a party is that you are there to enjoy yourself and to connect with others.

Combining partying and relationship-building may sound counterintuitive. But it works. I'll show you how throwing small parties in a strategic way can be the easiest method to make new friends and even boost your career.

The Perfect Party Formula

In the following chapters, you'll find everything you need to feel confident hosting your first party, including:

- Guest invitations: who to invite, how to invite them, and when to send the invitations to maximize RSVPs and minimize no-shows.

- **Scripts you can use:** my favorite and most effective email templates and event reminders to send after someone has RSVP'd. You'll learn how one of these messages makes people feel special, valued, and excited to attend— boosting your attendance rates above 80 percent.

- **Must-have supplies:** checklists with all you need to prepare for a seamless event.

- **Proven-to-work icebreakers:** the best conversation starters that I've found, why they work, and exactly how and when to use them.

Plus, plenty more tips and tricks to make your parties stress-free. From picking the best day of the week to knowing what to say when someone arrives early—and how to nicely ask people to leave at the end.

I used to be terrible at throwing parties. Then I discovered these specific tactics to get better at it. They are—and I can't stress this enough—incredibly easy to implement yourself.

You Can Do This!

Hosting parties that build big relationships is a skill you can learn. Everything you will read in this book has been tested and proven to work.

And sure, you might make a few mistakes. I've had mishaps along the way—like getting caught mid-shower when my first guest arrived early or hosting a party where only two people showed up.

But I've written this book so you don't have to repeat my mistakes.

Now let's go!

PART 1

The Basics

EXPECTATIONS   REALITY

CHAPTER 1

Why Host a Party

A NOTE FOR ADVANCED READERS

If you're ready to host your first party right now and want to get started immediately, skip ahead to "The Challenge" at the end of this chapter. Or, if you're still not sure about this whole "cocktail party" thing, keep reading. You'll learn about what happens at my parties and a few not-so-obvious reasons to host something like this.

When was the last time you made a new friend?

Maybe you do the same things with the same people every weekend. What else are you going to do? Maybe you've accepted the mindset of *I'm getting older. That's just how it is.*

But another way to think is *I'm getting older. Now is the best time to make a few new meaningful relationships.*

It's never too late to make new friends. There are people out there just like you: awesome, smart, motivated people who are a little lonely after work. Or they're bored of their same routine. They want to meet new people too.

Making Friends as an Adult Is Hard

It's hard to meet new people. It's even harder to make new friends and build relationships.

Science backs this up. I read about a study that found most American adults haven't made a new friend in over five years.[1] Another study showed that nearly half of US adults report feeling lonely and left out. It has reached, they say, "epidemic levels."[2]

Perhaps you still keep in touch with friends now from various parts of your life, but you wish you had an easy way to see them more often. Maybe you want to connect with certain

---

1   Zoya Gervis, "Why the Average American Hasn't Made a New Friend in 5 Years," *New York Post*, May 9, 2019, https://nypost.com/2019/05/09/why-the-average-american-hasnt-made-a-new-friend-in-5-years or www.party.pro/footnotes
2   "Many Americans Are Lonely, and Gen Z Most of All, Study Finds," CBS News, May 3, 2018, https://cbsnews.com/news/many-americans-are-lonely-and-gen-z-most-of-all-study-finds or www.party.pro/footnotes

people in your career, but you don't want it to seem awkward. Or maybe you just want to make some new friends, like millions of others, and you want more out of life.

Well, heck yes. You can do all of those things. But it stinks that no one, and I mean *no one*, teaches adults how to make new friends in a straightforward, practical manner—until now.

Over the past few years, I've heard from tons of people who shared similar frustrations. That was the case for a woman who came to one of my parties and was so inspired that she now hosts her own. I wrote this book to give people like Lindsey (and you) a roadmap to create new connections.

Lindsey's Story: A Decision That Changed Her Life

Lindsey Martin is a shy thirty-one-year-old. Originally from Texas, she's now been living in New York City for ten years. Her life changed when she made the decision to host her first party.

Lindsey owns and runs a digital marketing company. Her job requires a lot of screen time, and she has little face time with her audience or customers. She found herself craving human connection and wanting to make new friends that would inspire her. She decided to throw a party where she could meet some of her readers and clients.

Lindsey started by hosting women's networking events. At the first one, she was nervous and felt like she had no idea what she was doing. But she followed the formula from an early draft of this book and did it anyway. Her first party was a success: more than fifteen guests came, and many of them met new friends, received job leads, or found a workout buddy. People kept telling her how fun her party was and asking when the next one would be.

Today Lindsey's events are so popular that she has to limit the number of attendees. Others think of her more often too. People invite her to birthday parties and gym workouts. Her social calendar is overflowing with opportunities that excite her and make her feel connected. She also developed true friendships. She even met one of her best friends at one of her parties, and together they started a business club that meets every month.

Lindsey finds value from hosting parties. She loves the feeling of helping people. She also developed new business relationships that have brought her cool projects, like a big book launch campaign for a fashion icon. All of this came from investing time in a single skill: hosting parties.

Lindsey's hosting experience is not without challenges. As an introvert, she doesn't feel natural commanding a room. But this self-awareness reminds her that it is hard for people to meet others when they're shy. By stepping out of her comfort zone to host, she gives her guests a chance to meet new people while simultaneously boosting her own confidence.

Most Networking Events Are Terrible

I've been to lots of terrible networking events. I'm sure you know the kind...I'd walk into a packed bar and stand there feeling like an outsider. The music was so loud that conversation was impossible. There was no easy way to meet people because nobody was facilitating things or making introductions. I'd usually get a drink just to keep busy, then have forced "So what do you do?" conversations with a few random people.

I rarely made any exciting new connections at these kinds of events. Something about it was way too transactional and inauthentic. After an hour, I'd normally leave and swear off trying to "build my network" forever. These things were such a waste of time.

But it doesn't have to be that way!

What's Different about My Parties?

My party formula brings a totally different approach. It's definitely not a networking event, but compared to most casual gatherings with friends and colleagues, there's a *lot* of structure. For example:

- Everyone wears a name tag so it's easy to meet (Chapter 5).

- You know who will be there beforehand (Chapter 9).

- The party feels friendly and warm when you arrive (Chapter 11).

- The host frequently facilitates introductions to help you start new conversations (Chapter 12).

While you might fear imposing a structure like this onto a small party, I found that structure makes things easier. It liberates your guests from uncertainty. It lets them get comfortable and encourages them to chat and meet new people.

But my party formula is not so structured that it feels like a formal business meeting. Far from it. Here's a typical party:

Everyone comes into a room where the energy is high. I'm standing by the door and greet guests with a huge smile. They each get a name tag, and another friend of mine shows them the makeshift bar area to fix a drink.

A few days earlier, I sent out a reminder message with short notes about many of the guests. That helps people recognize a few of the names on the tags to start conversations. There's a healthy air of curiosity among everyone to meet new people.

Soon I make a playful little noise to bring the room to attention. I ask everyone to circle up and then quickly lead a round of icebreakers to make newcomers feel included. These icebreakers happen fast. Everyone goes around the room and says their name, a little about what they do during the day, and something else interesting or fun about themselves. After the icebreaker, the room comes alive as new conversations form.

Guests pop around to meet a few different people. Thirty minutes later, I lead another iteration of icebreakers. New people have arrived, and the room is getting more crowded.

Two hours fly by. Now, new friends who didn't know anyone when they arrived have met several interesting people whom they genuinely look forward to following up with. I warmly usher people out and some are surprised to get home before 10:00 p.m.

Attendees to my party are inspired by the people they met. They've never been to a cocktail party like that before. It reminds them that meeting new people feels great, and they look forward to the next one.

The Benefits of Being the Host

At this point, you're probably thinking: *Hosting something like that sounds great, but it also sounds like a lot of work. Is it actually worth it?* I'm biased, but the short answer is *yes!* Here are three big ways that hosting cocktail parties will change your life:

1. Meet Awesome People

We know that approaching new people to develop a personal or business relationship can be intimidating. Even terrifying. I've avoided asking someone out for a friendly coffee or a drink because I was afraid of being rejected. I thought, *What if they say no?*

Then I found a solution: invite them to my party. Compared to a dinner or a coffee meeting, a cocktail party is a fun way to get to know somebody. It is a small commitment and an easy invitation to say yes to.

After asking hundreds of people, I've consistently received a positive response to the question "Can I invite you to my next cocktail party?" Everyone appreciates being invited to a party.

2. Boost Your Reputation

I don't know how to say this without it sounding like a power grab, so I'll just say it: hosting parties makes you more popular. For me, cocktail parties have led to business opportunities (like new clients), introductions (like amazing friends), and invitations (like fun events).

The same thing will happen to you. Here's how it works: You'll get introduced to friends of friends as someone who hosts a great party. Everyone wants to know someone like this. Because you're the one who has the courage to bring people together, you'll start to build your reputation as a natural connector. You'll get introduced to interesting people—sometimes when you least expect it. It's one of the most surprising follow-on benefits new hosts tell me about.

3. Strengthen Relationships

Have you ever wondered what your old friends are doing? Or how about your acquaintances or colleagues at work to whom you say, "We should hang out!" but then never actually do? Hosting a party makes it easy to hang out with people like this.

Compare the numbers: Coffee meetings are one-on-one and take about an hour. Dinner parties often have four to eight guests and can last an entire evening. But a 2-hour cocktail party lets you connect with fifteen people all at once. In the time it takes to watch a movie, you can improve your relationships with a room full of people. It is the most efficient and effective way I've found to strengthen many different connections.

THE STRENGTH OF WEAK TIES

You'll be exposed to new opportunities—ones you maybe can't even imagine—when you host parties. Research shows that most people find out about new jobs and opportunities through "weak ties"; the people we see occasionally, perhaps only once or twice a year.

Sociologist Mark Granovetter coined the term in his 1973 paper, "The Strength of Weak Ties." According to Wired, Granovetter noted that "people were nearly three times as likely to have found their job through a 'personal contact' than through an advertisement, headhunter, or other 'formal means.'"[1]

Referencing the same study, Business Insider reported that "acquaintances are more likely to know something

---

[1]   Jonah Lehrer, "Weak Ties, Twitter and Revolution," Wired, September 29, 2010, www.wired.com/2010/09/weak-ties-twitter-and-revolutions or www.party.pro/footnotes

you don't. They represent social power—and the more acquaintances you have, the more powerful you are."[1]

Your Guests Will Benefit Too

This party formula works because it benefits everyone who attends. You'll give real value to the friends, acquaintances, and colleagues you invite when you help them meet new people. Creating new connections is one of the most impactful and generous things you can do for another person.

A few guests from one of my parties later shared the direct ways they benefitted by attending:

- Amy Ling Lin, owner of several nail salons, met a consultant who she then hired to help grow her sales.

- Ben Fisher, a product designer and Shopify consultant, was invited to an immersive classical music concert after he met the organizer. He called it the highlight of his year.

---

1   Aimee Groth, "Gladwell on Why We're Connected to More Powerful People than We Think," *Business Insider*, July 14, 2011, www.businessinsider.com/malcolm-gladwell-tipping-point-connectors-2011-7 or www.party.pro/footnotes

- Richard Murray, a financial advisor, landed a big new investment account.

Who knows what connections your guests will make at your parties! I'm still waiting to introduce two people who fall in love and get married. Maybe you'll pull it off before I do.

The Challenge

Before we get into the nitty-gritty of party hosting and exactly how to do it, I want you to take up my challenge. It's simple:

Commit to hosting your first party three weeks from now.

Pick a Monday, Tuesday, or Wednesday night three weeks from now and save it on your calendar.

Pick a Monday, Tuesday, or Wednesday night. Set the date and put it in your calendar. You'll learn why these days work best in Chapter 2. For now, simply make the commitment and let your party-hosting adventure officially begin.

A Message for Skeptics

Perhaps you're still a bit skeptical. Some people wonder what will happen if nobody shows up, especially on a Tuesday night. They worry that their party will be boring, people will leave early, and then their friends will think less of them. (*This will not happen. I promise.*)

Some feel too introverted to face such a daunting task. They think that hosting a party takes too much work, it is too much stress, or they're too busy to do it during the week. They worry it will be expensive and cost hundreds of dollars. (*It won't.*)

Just thinking about this challenge and who you should invite might make you feel vulnerable.

Look, I've felt all of those things, and I understand where you're coming from. I also know that there comes a time to say "screw it" and just do it.

It's OK to be nervous about throwing a party. Use this book as an excuse to host your first one, then blame me if it goes poorly. Really. Say this when you invite people later: "I'm reading a book about how to host a happy hour. I've never done one before, and now I want to try it out." Or say, "This guy Nick that I saw on the internet always posts about these 2-hour cocktail parties." This gives you some space to practice and an easy punching bag (me) if anything is a little awkward.

For now, just commit to hosting a small cocktail party for a few of your friends. Focus only on this first party using the examples in this book.

Parties aren't hard to throw. If you want to become a better host, you can. I felt like a total amateur at the start, and so did everyone else I've helped. I've got your back now.

In the next chapter, we'll dig into the details.

A NOTE ABOUT THE PHRASE "COCKTAIL PARTY"

The phrase "cocktail party" is the best that I've found to quickly describe the atmosphere that these events are meant to create. Cocktail parties have always been small events for people to get together and socialize in a fun way. The cocktails and snacks are only there to set the scene. It's never been about the drinks—it's always been about the people.

In the first few years of hosting my gatherings, I didn't drink alcohol. I hosted cocktail parties but didn't actually know how to make a cocktail. And you know what? It didn't matter. People weren't coming to my events for fancy drinks. They still don't.

Throughout this book, I'll use terms like cocktail party and event and gathering interchangeably. You could also call it a mixer, a get-together, a happy hour, or whatever term feels natural and appropriate to you. They all convey the same idea with the same purpose and results.

☑ CHAPTER CHECKLIST

☐   Accept my challenge and plan to host your first party three weeks from now.

☐   If you want an accountability partner, email the date you picked for your first party to nick@party.pro. I'll try to check in with you along the way.

CHAPTER 2

When to Host Your Party

There is a good reason why you should select a date three weeks away for your first party: it will give time to build your guest list.

The Party Runway

Think of a runway at an airport. It exists to give the plane time to build up speed and take off. In the context of hosting a party, the runway gives you plenty of time to invite people. Plus, advance notice makes it more likely that your guests will have an open schedule and be able to attend.

A three-week runway allows you to do most of the work in advance to guarantee great attendance.

The runway also gives you time to buy a few necessary supplies like basic drinks and some snacks. But don't panic about preparation yet. We're just making a runway right now, not a whole airport.

Three weeks is the sweet spot. It provides you with plenty of time to build a solid list of RSVPs. You'll message a few close connections, create a simple online event page, lock in those first RSVPs, and then send invites to other prospective guests. Upcoming chapters will cover each of these steps in detail. For now, just know that a long party runway will increase your party's attendance and decrease your stress.

How Not to Plan a Party

As I mentioned, I haven't always been a natural host. Years ago, on my journey to becoming a party professional, I was attending a mindfulness class in New York City. It was there that I met Olivia, a friend of a friend who was successful in the fashion industry. I loved her style and was incredibly curious about her world and network. After chatting for a few minutes, I knew that I wanted to see her again.

What better way to get to know her than by inviting her to a cocktail party I was thinking of organizing?

She was excited. We added each other on social media, and I said I'd add her to the Facebook event I had already made for the party. To my delight, she said she couldn't wait to come. Unfortunately, I screwed up.

Yes, I was *thinking* about organizing a party, but I hadn't done any of the groundwork. I stood there outside the class with calming Zen music playing in the background, and as I added her to the Facebook event on my phone, I realized what was about to happen. I felt a sudden flush of embarrassment.

I hadn't yet reached out to my core group of trusted friends and colleagues (you'll learn more about what this is and why it is important soon). The event I was inviting her to showed only one other confirmed attendee: me.

From her perspective, it must have looked as though I was pulling a sleazy trick to get her to come to my apartment.

When I got home, I knew I needed to put together a party with less than a week's notice. I invited as many friends as I could, and I begged them to attend. I rushed out and bought supplies.

It was a scramble, but I did it. Olivia attended and had a great time and we ended up becoming friends. Thankfully I didn't look like too much of a weirdo. I was lucky that time. But the whole experience was way more stressful than it needed to be.

 Do: decrease the party stress by planning ahead.

 Do: invite interesting new people you meet.

 Don't: invite them before you've prepared the party runway.

The Best Day Criteria

Host your first party on a non-busy weeknight. Monday, Tuesday, or Wednesday nights work best for me. Choose a day when most people you plan to invite are probably available. This makes it easier for them to say yes to your invitation.

I always avoid Thursday, Friday, and Saturday nights because I don't want to risk schedule conflicts for my guests. Sunday tends to be a family or rest day, so I skip that day too. And steer clear of long weekends and holidays. All of these are what I call "heavyweight" days.

 Do: Monday, Tuesday, or Wednesday night.

 Don't: Thursday, Friday, Saturday, or Sunday night.

 Don't: long weekends or holidays.

Heavyweight Days: Why They're Your Enemy

My friend Steve decided to host his first party on one of the most heavyweight days of the year: New Year's Eve. New Year's Eve is like the World Championship of Parties. It's not the night to throw a party unless you *really* know what you're doing and plan well in advance.

To make matters worse, Steve sent out his invitations by mass email using an online service. I found mine in my spam folder in late December. He didn't even text me—one of his best friends—to invite me individually or remind me to RSVP.

When I called him, it was clear he was stressed. He'd invested a lot of time and money into his planning and was worried about whether people were going to show up. His hosting confidence was shaken before the event even happened.

 PARTY PRO TIP

> Don't try to compete with busy social calendars.
> Host your party when people are less likely to
> have plans.

Steve managed to pull it off, but the party didn't live up to its potential. There were fewer guests than he'd hoped for, and he'd spent too much time and money renting a space and getting decorations. You don't want this to happen to you, so don't pick a heavyweight day for your first party.

Avoid schedule conflicts for your guests. Host your party on a less-busy day.

ASK THE PARTY PROFESSIONAL

Q: Should parties always take place on weekdays and at night?

A: I've found these days and times are easier to organize for a two-hour event. People's schedules tend to be more flexible during the week and after work. But these recommendations aren't set in stone. What worked in my research in a big city may not work for you. Those with kids or who live in smaller towns might prefer to gather on weekends. Plan an event you feel comfortable hosting, and be thoughtful if departing from my formula—especially for your first few parties.

Drinks Only—No Dinner Parties

Do not position this as a dinner party. Dinner parties are too hard for new hosts to manage. They take a lot of work. You must finely curate the guest list, order lots of supplies, cook the food, lead the entire conversation, and entertain longer.

 PARTY PRO TIP

Serve drinks and snacks only. Make your first party a success by keeping it simple.

ASK THE PARTY PROFESSIONAL

Q: Can I use the formula in this book for a party I've already scheduled next week? Like a sports event, birthday party, or work function?

A: I don't recommend it, and here's why: your guests didn't sign up for a structured cocktail party. They RSVP'd to watch football or whatever you invited them to do. If you greet them with nachos and name tags, they're going to be confused and might not be willing participants. The best way to learn this formula is by planning a party specifically for the purpose of practicing what's in the book.

But if you're reading this to help you upgrade a party only a few days away, you can still do several key things to make your gathering better. Jump ahead to Chapter 5 to see the magic of name tags, then skip to Chapter 9 to learn about best practices for your reminder messages. I've posted more thoughts about how to improve an upcoming party at www.party.pro/tips.

I hosted dozens of dinner parties in my quest to find the perfect formula to build relationships. But I stopped doing them when I realized that cocktail parties are so much easier to master. Cocktail parties will give you the same or even better relationship-building results than dinner parties because you can do them more often and you can invite more people. The impact is the same and the conversations are often livelier. Keep it simple and don't do dinner.

What Time Works Best?

Start at 7:00 p.m. and end at 9:00 p.m.

An event that starts at 7:00 p.m. gives people time to finish their workday and come straight to your party or eat dinner before arriving. They also go home early, so you can do it on a weekday without feeling guilty.

While 7:00 p.m. to 9:00 p.m. works best for me, I know a few hosts who throw parties from 8:00 to 10:00 or even 6:30 to 8:30. After your first party, you can experiment to find the time block that works best for you and your community.

If you want to have a bit of fun with the start and end time, you can pick a random minute around 7:00 p.m. and 9:00 p.m. Sol Orwell, the co-founder of the scientific research database Examine.com, started hosting parties because he wanted to commiserate with his fellow entrepreneurs in Toronto. He always uses quirky start and end times like 6:57 p.m. to 9:02 p.m. It sets his parties apart from boring networking events, and I have a hunch the novelty might encourage people to show up on time.

Party People in Action: Nagina Sethi Abdulla

Founder of MasalaBody.com in Jersey City, New Jersey

Nick: Why did you decide to start hosting parties?

Nagina: I wanted to feel like my town was "home" and that my kids and I could enjoy our time and have a community to learn from and spend time with. I moved here when they were in preschool. With my work and entrepreneurship-focused lifestyle, I had not made time to meet new people and make friends.

Nick: What have you gained by hosting parties?

Nagina: I created so many new connections. When I go out in town—to the store, a restaurant, or a school event—it's much more common that I see someone I know. I also gained confidence that I'm adding value to my community.

Nick: What's the biggest challenge or fear you've faced hosting parties?

Nagina: Before my first party, I had a real fear about putting myself out there and hosting. There was so much possible rejection if people didn't come. What surprised me was that when I invited people personally like this book teaches, they got really excited to come. Even if they were busy or said no, they appreciated my invitation.

Provide Clear Start and Finish Times

Two hours is the perfect length of time for a cocktail party. It's long enough for people to meet and talk, yet short enough to prevent the party from fizzling out. Keep your party concise in order to:

- Encourage guests to show up on time and not be fashionably late.

- Make your parties easier to say yes to, especially on a weekday.

- Reduce your stress by setting expectations for when guests should leave.

The clear ending time tells guests that your party isn't an opportunity for a blowout or a crazy long night. Everyone needs to get up for work, family, or school the next day.

You might worry about what to do at the end. If your guests want to hang out and continue socializing after your party is over, congratulations! That means you've done a great job creating connections. But that chatter and reluctance to leave doesn't mean you need to continue hosting. Recommend a nearby bar or restaurant that guests can go to, then finish the party at the time you stated in the invitation. You're free to join them at the next venue or tidy up your space and rest. You'll learn more about how to end your party gracefully and on a high note in Chapter 14.

☑ CHAPTER CHECKLIST

☐ Confirm your date. Ideally a Monday, Tuesday, or Wednesday evening three weeks out.

☐ Set your two-hour time block. I suggest 7:00 p.m. to 9:00 p.m.

☐ Don't invite anyone just yet. You'll learn who to invite and exactly how to invite them in Chapter 4.

CHAPTER 3

Where to Host Your Party

Have you ever been to a "barty"? You probably have, even if you're not familiar with the word.

A barty is a birthday party or other special event held at a bar.

Whenever I get invited to a barty, a little piece of me dies inside. I feel like the good luck leprechaun of party hosting has just lost his pot of gold.

A Barty is the Enemy

Here are some of the reasons why a barty is a major missed opportunity:

- They're noisy, so it's hard to talk.

- You can't control the aesthetics of the space or who is allowed in.

- Ordering drinks is transactional, the opposite of welcoming.

Barties usually lack clear structure and rules. Crowded bars can inhibit connecting. We miss out on making new friends and strengthening relationships with the people we know.

Many people are tempted to throw parties at a bar because it seems so easy. Resist this temptation. Host your first party at a venue where you feel confident and can control as many variables as possible.

Why You Should Host at Home

The best place to host your party is at your home. Your house or apartment is instantly personal. It's a chance to break out of your work and online identity.

When you invite people into your home, you offer them the chance to visit your personal space. You reveal more about who you are, especially in a world where digital interaction dominates. A lot of people appreciate this vulnerability. You feel more relatable to them. It will help your guests see you in a positive light, and they will forgive any aspects of your home that aren't "perfect." They won't care if your house is small, plain, or a little messy. They're coming to your party to enjoy themselves and to meet new people, not to pass judgment on your dust bunnies.

Host your party in your own house or apartment because:

- You'll have more confidence in your own space.

- You can control variables like noise levels and costs.

- Your guests will appreciate you more because of how intimate and generous it feels.

Host your party at home for these reasons. The crown is optional.

Common Objections to Hosting at Home

When I suggest hosting a cocktail party at home, many people resist the idea. Some live far away from friends and worry that no one will make the effort to come to their event. Others worry their kids' playroom is messy, their guest bedroom isn't finished, they don't have the right furniture in the dining room, or their apartment is too small.

If you feel this way, your concerns are normal. But the location, size, and state of your home aren't as big of a deal as you think. People aren't going to judge you harshly if your home is a little cluttered or you don't have a huge, fancy apartment. Guests are more likely to appreciate your authenticity. You'll have more confidence too, being in your own space. You'll build relationships better and faster, and you'll set yourself apart when you host at home.

Small Is OK

New York City has many tiny living spaces. My friend Phillip has hosted twenty people in his two-hundred-square-foot apartment. I've seen his photos of a group of people crammed into a kitchen the size of a yoga mat. They were all smiling.

A small space makes an event feel intimate and special. I hosted at least ninety parties in my New York City studio apartment. It consisted of one main room with a built-in kitchen the size of the galley you'd find on a small boat. It's tiny but functional.

If Phillip and I can host parties in a small space, so can you.

Party People in Action: Danielle Schulz

Ballet Dancer at The Metropolitan Opera
in Brooklyn, New York

Nick: Why did you decide to start hosting parties?
Danielle: I wanted to blend my artistic group of friends with my husband's MBA circle.

Nick: What's the biggest challenge or fear you've faced hosting parties?
Danielle: I thought that a modestly sized one-bedroom apartment in Brooklyn would deter people from attending, but that hasn't been the case. I find last-minute cancellations and no-shows frustrating, even disheartening. But it's bound to happen, and I remind myself not to take it personally.

Nick: What have you gained by hosting parties?
Danielle: Hosting these parties is all about connecting and nurturing relationships for me. One of the best compliments I received after a party was, "For two

↘

whole hours I didn't see a single person break out their phone. Everyone was enthralled in conversation and truly connected with one another." I've also used these parties to practice and increase my confidence in facilitating group interaction and making more corporate connections for my business.

Nick: Do you have any advice to new hosts?
Danielle: I was nervous about the name tags. To help ease the awkwardness, I had guests write their favorite food underneath their name. This created a built-in icebreaker and made it feel more fun. People love talking about food.

When Hosting at Home Isn't Possible

For 95 percent of the people I've advised, hosting at home is a realistic option despite their initial objections. For the other 5 percent, it simply isn't. Here's why:

- A family member requires care at home, which makes it complicated to invite a lot of people over.

- They do not have an elevator, and they want their parties to be wheelchair accessible.

- They live with unfriendly roommates or in a multifamily situation. It makes it hard to know when the house will be free.

You can still throw parties even if hosting at home is not a possibility. The easiest and most common solution is to find a friend or colleague who will let you use their home for your party. Other options include:

- A park.

- A library or community center.

- Your apartment or neighborhood common space or game room.

- Your office.

 PARTY PRO TIP

Name tags are especially important when you're hosting an event outside your home. In a shared space, name tags become a visual unifier for your group. They'll make it easier to identify your guests.

See more tips and tricks for hosting outside your home, including additional venue ideas, at www.party.pro/venues.

Nia's Story: Bloody Marys and Brunch

Nia, a fitness instructor in Texas, chose to host her first event at a local restaurant. She was worried that her house was too small. She felt her home wasn't located in a prestigious or trendy neighborhood and didn't have the layout to successfully host a group, which she thought should be a large dining table that could seat twelve or more people.

I told Nia these things didn't matter as much as she thought. I tried to tell her that **sitting down is kryptonite to a successful event** and that it would cause her icebreakers to drone on forever and kill the energy level.

Standing allows for more dynamic interactions. Sitting keeps people trapped in conversation.

Nia continued with her plan and hosted her first event at the local restaurant. She called the party "Bloody Marys and Brunch." The brunch went relatively well. But doing it at the restaurant saddled her with logistical hurdles outside her control:

- Splitting checks between twelve different people was a major distraction. It prevented the event from ending on a high note.

- The room was noisy. It was hard to hear people at normal conversation levels. Talking to people more than one or two chairs away was impossible.

- When Nia started her first round of icebreakers, her guests were already seated. There wasn't an easy space in the restaurant to have everyone stand up and gather. This made it hard for Nia to keep the icebreakers short. They ended up taking almost forty minutes to complete.

When Nia later took the leap and hosted an event in her home, she quickly realized how much better it was. Nobody cared about the size of her house. None of her guests snuck into her guest bedroom to check whether it was clean. They were simply happy to be there. People could move around. Conversations flowed more freely. Everyone had a great time, including Nia. She emailed me later:

"The party I hosted at my home was so much better. My home does not reflect where I'm at in my career. But I put that fear away, and now I have new best friends and several new acquaintances. Also, no one cares! There are so many people with bigger and better decorated homes who don't have the confidence to host. People look up to those who host."

☑ CHAPTER CHECKLIST

☐ Write down all of your concerns about hosting at home. Address each one. Know that you're making the right decision to host at home.

☐ Believe in your decision, recommit to your party date, and have confidence that you're doing the smart thing by hosting at home.

☐ If you're unable to host at home, try partnering with a friend who will let you use their space. Or host your party at a park, library, community center, or office. See www.party.pro/venues for more resources.

CHAPTER 4

Who to Invite

Your first party should feel easy to host. Start by inviting close friends, colleagues, and neighbors.

My First Party

I moved to New York City just shy of my twenty-sixth birthday. That became my excuse to muster up the courage and host my first-ever New York City party.

I didn't drink alcohol at the time, so I knew I didn't want to celebrate my birthday at a bar. I wanted to do something different. After checking with my roommates, I threw my birthday party at our shared apartment in Brooklyn, reserving the kitchen area as a party space.

I started by inviting my friends from college because I assumed they'd come. I messaged a few of them first to check their availability for the proposed date and time of my party. Once I had confirmations from five of them, I had a lot more confidence. I knew that at least those five people would be there.

Next, I began inviting more people, including neighbors and friends of friends. I followed the blog of a woman named Mallory Blair and thought she was a great writer. We'd traded messages for a while online. Since I knew my core group of college friends were already coming to the party, I could confidently say, "My friends and I are getting together on December 8 for my birthday. Do you want to come?"

Mallory was happy to receive an invitation and came to the party. She had a lot of fun and connected well with my friends. But since we were only passing acquaintances, I would never have had the confidence to ask Mallory to hang out one-on-one.

Today Mallory is a highly successful business owner with her own PR agency in New York City and Los Angeles. I count her as one of my best friends. We even became roommates for a few years. She hired me and my company to run two team building events for her agency. All of that would never have happened had I not first confirmed my close friends and then had the courage to invite Mallory to my party.

Your Core Group

At my first party, my friends from college formed what I call a core group.

Any time you host an event, always invite your core group first. These are your reliable and supportive friends and colleagues. They already know and like you. You can ask them for a favor or invite them to something without overthinking it. Because you already have a relationship, they're likely to say yes to your invitation.

Your core group will be an essential piece of your party puzzle. They'll show up and make you look good. They'll laugh at your jokes and be your party cheerleaders. They're people with whom you feel comfortable. They're also your support team and safety net.

In the next chapter, you'll see the exact words to use when inviting your core group. You'll first check whether they are available for your party. If they are, you'll ask them to confirm that they would like to come.

Inviting your core group first is a way to stack the deck for a successful party. Their RSVPs will build your confidence as a host to know that good people are coming. Then you will start inviting more people to your party.

Stack the deck for your party by inviting your core group first.

After you get five confirmations from people in your core group, you can begin to cast a wider net of party attendees, like other work colleagues and friends. I use the term "great guests" to refer to everyone you invite after your core group. It sounds better than "non-core guests" or "other people I work with." This name represents who these people are to you: guests who it would be great to have at your party.

Creating a Core Group When You Don't Have One

If you just moved to a new city, or if you haven't been very sociable in the past, don't worry. Making friends and building a core group can be easier than you think.

Richard Garand in Calgary, Canada posted notes around his apartment complex inviting all his neighbors to his first party. It's not a core group in the traditional sense, but it still got him enough RSVPs to have the confidence to invite more people to his first gathering.

Try these ideas to create a core group when you don't have one:

- Join a local club for something you're interested in, like volleyball, poker, or Toastmasters.

- Look up event calendars on local media or Facebook groups to find interesting things to attend.

- Volunteer with a charity or religious organization.

- Attend Meetups (find them at www.meetup.com) especially for people who are new in town or looking to make friends.

Here are some more suggestions from people who read early drafts of this book:

"Look at organizations for ex-pats like InterNations. They have groups in over four hundred cities. I find ex-pats can be more open to connecting. Unlike locals, they don't have established networks and might have just moved to a city."

—Judhajit De

"I have invited a few very distant relatives that live in town to parties. For example, my mother-in-law's cousin's daughter. She's someone I met once at a big family event, seemed cool, and it turned out we could be friends in addition to extremely distant in-laws."

—Alex Gates

"For women looking to meet new friends, try the Bumble app and use the Bumble BFF setting. It's a great way to connect. I met a number of new people using it and invited them to my parties."

—Gena Stanley

"Join a recreational sports league in your area. I play on soccer teams and have made many friends over the years. My own Party Pro Tip: To maximize the opportunity of meeting people, play kickball because that sport has the largest teams."

—Seth Hanes

"Reach out to people from your yoga, boxing, or gym classes. Invite the coaches and instructors too."

—Rui Zhang

How Many People to Invite

For your first party, aim for fifteen confirmed guests. I've found that fifteen people at a cocktail party gives the best balance. With fewer people—like seven or eight—you're more likely to get trapped in a single group conversation or have an uncomfortable silence in the room. The connections will be less free-flowing, and the room will lack energy. Any no-shows will hit you hard.

On the other hand, if you have too many guests—say, thirty—managing the logistics becomes a big challenge. There's a lot of energy with a lot of people, but your party can descend into carnage. You might wake up in a pile of smelly wine bottles with rotten pizza crusts on the floor and a court summons for local noise violations. (It happens to the best of us.)

After your first few parties, you can experiment with hosting more or less than fifteen people. See how you enjoy the experience and adapt this formula later to fit your style.

Invite More Than You Need

Over-inviting is a natural part of party planning. If you want fifteen people to come to your party, you'll need to invite twenty to thirty people total.

It's unlikely that everyone will say yes. That's normal. Is it because they don't like you? Maybe! But probably not. Try to remember: people have a lot going on in their lives. I still frequently experience the feeling of rejection when guests turn down my invitations. Try not to take it personally when this happens. And besides, when have you ever liked someone less because they invited you to a party?

ASK THE PARTY PROFESSIONAL

Q: What if only three people show up and my party is terribly boring?

A: This is a common fear for new hosts. It may have even happened to you in the past. But fear not. When you give yourself a long runway, secure your core group first, and use the framework from this book, you'll have plenty of time to build up your guest list, generate excitement, and then guarantee attendance for a fun party that almost everyone shows up for.

If you're someone who likes being over-prepared and you're still worried about what will happen if only a few people show up to your party, just have a board or card game on hand. Pick one that you like and that is easy to learn. I like the card games SET and Monopoly Deal. For a list of other games that work well at parties, see www.party.pro/games.

Who to Invite: Your First Party

It's fine to have a seemingly random group of connections at your party. In fact, it's what will make your event special and allow your guests to meet new and interesting people. The common thread is that everyone knows you.

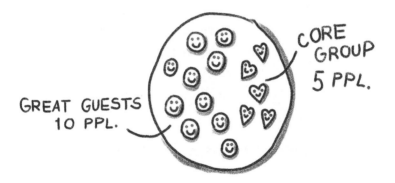

Your first party should have fifteen attendees. It will be a mix of different people you know, including great guests and your core group.

Follow these guidelines for picking who to invite to your first party:

Do: invite friends, neighbors, classmates, colleagues, and their significant others.

 Don't: invite important new relationships or critical work contacts.

DON'T INVITE VIPS...YET

Some people become so excited to host their first party that they rush to send invitations. They reach out to everyone they'd like to have at their party, including big business contacts and new romantic interests.

It's great that you're excited to show off your new hosting skills. You should be. But pace yourself. Don't start your hosting journey by inviting people who intimidate you or who you badly want to impress. Focus your guest list now on friends and colleagues. When your first party is a low-stakes affair, you'll avoid the stress of trying to impress VIP guests. Invite them later after this first practice party.

Who to Invite: Second and Third Parties

When you create your guest list for your second and third parties, then you can stretch yourself and cast a wider net of guests. Invite the same people from your first party, plus a few more people you don't know as well or haven't seen in a while. This includes the following:

- Friends of friends

- Former colleagues and classmates

- Colleagues in other departments

- Sales professionals or service staff at your favorite local spots

You can also invite new people you meet. Liz Schwarzbach, a pharmacologist and business executive in Manhattan, says that her metric for whether to invite someone to an event is this:

> "When I meet someone new, I ask myself: do I want to continue the conversation or see them again? If the answer is yes, then they would make a great guest for one of my parties."

Be mindful of keeping a genuine interest in your guest list. You're not trying to use and abuse your old and new friends in a self-serving manner. This is what gives networking a bad name.

Do: invite new acquaintances who you would be excited to see again or continue a conversation with.

 Don't: purely build a guest list based on "Who can I benefit from right now?"

Every new person you meet becomes a potential party invitation.

How to Grow Your Guest List

If you're eager to grow your guest list, here are some things to try:

- Invite everyone you might want to see again. Follow Liz's advice. Invite anyone you meet that you might like to talk to again. Your guest list will naturally grow. It doesn't have to be some big, grand invitation. If you meet someone neat at work or in the grocery store, just mention you're having a party soon, and ask if you can invite them. If they say yes, take their contact details. If they say no, what's the harm? Either take their details and invite them to your next party, or continue on with your day.

- Think about the people you regularly interact with in town. This could be your barista or your workout instructor or the service staff at your favorite restaurant. Give them an invite.

- Log on to Facebook, LinkedIn, or another social network you use. Search for friends or colleagues who live in your city. We often forget about our loose connections and acquaintances we've already made through these networks.

- Send your core group members a personalized message asking them to bring a friend to your party. Give them at least one week's notice. For bonus points, provide them with a little script like this to make it easy to share:

I'd like to ask a favor: Will you help me out and bring a friend or colleague to my party? You can send them this message: "My friend Nick is hosting a cocktail party on Wednesday the 8th at 7 p.m. It will be fun! May I share your info with him to send you the information?"

- Follow up a few days later to ask each person in your core group who they are going to bring. It is important to ask them to "bring a friend," not just "invite a friend." When you explicitly state that you want them to bring someone, it implies you want them to follow through.

- Make a list of "super connectors" in your town and invite one or two. This could include real estate agents, salespeople, fundraising staff at a nonprofit, and recruiters. These folks have huge networks and are often receptive to invitations to meet new people.

Party People in Action: Mary Beth Yale
Literary Consultant in Mexico City, Mexico

Nick: Why did you decide to start hosting parties?
Mary Beth: Successfully hosting fun parties was a longtime goal of mine. I always imagined I'd be a

sophisticated adult once I did it. I often meet new people, and it's a bit overwhelming to plan a coffee or one-on-one meal. Parties are a sustainable and fun way for me to get a lot of great people in one room.

Nick: Who do you invite to your parties?
Mary Beth: I've hosted two parties so far. At the first, I invited a lot of my neighbors. For the second, I invited newcomers to the city. For example, I recently knocked somebody's drink over at a bar. He wouldn't let me buy him a new drink. So, I invited him to my next cocktail party. Turns out he is an author, and we have a friend in common who lives in Italy. It was awesome to see my friends making connections and to be the one facilitating it.

The Advantage of a Diverse Guest List

As you become more comfortable as a host, reach out to people who are less like yourself. When I throw a party, I focus on adding occupational diversity to my guest list. I invite friends who work in banking, dancing, and education in addition to those in museums, technology, and marketing.

I like what Joan Crawford said in 1971 in her book *My Way of Life* about entertaining people at home:

> "The best parties are a wild mixture. Take some corporation presidents, add...a bearded painter, a professional jockey, your visiting friends from Brussels, a politician, a hairdresser, and a professor of physics, toss them all together, and try to get them to stop talking long enough to eat! It's especially important to have all age groups. I've never noticed any generation gap...all the younger people I know are bright and attractive and have something to say and they dress like human beings. They love to listen, too. They make wonderful guests."

The idea of having a diverse attendee list is timeless. Conversations at your party will be more unexpected and interesting.

Tyler's Story: New Town, New Core Group

Tyler Vawser is the father of three young kids, a vice president at an education software company, and an extremely successful party host. (He's the guy I mentioned in the Introduction.) Before he moved from New York City to Little Rock, Arkansas, I sat down with him and explained my party formula. We talked about why he wanted to become a host.

Tyler was moving to a new city where he didn't know any-
one. He didn't yet have a core group of friends. His only
contacts would be his wife's family, who had been born and
raised there. He wanted to build his own network and land
a great job.

When Tyler arrived in Little Rock, he heard from friends
back in New York about a woman named Erica who had
also moved to Arkansas and hosted parties in the area. Tyler
reached out to her and asked if she wanted to co-host a small
cocktail party with him. Not only did Erica say yes, but she
invited a number of people she'd gotten to know while living
in Little Rock.

Tyler relied on Erica to bring in a core group of friends, and
their first event together was a success. Even better, by part-
nering with her, Tyler began to develop his own core group.

Since then, Tyler has gone on to meet dozens of new people
through hosting his own parties. He even secured his exec-
utive job through someone he met at one of his events. The
founder and a few other employees had been invited to his
cocktail parties. When it was time to grow their People &
Culture team, they thought of Tyler.

"There's a serendipity to these parties," Tyler told me. "I like
seeing others make connections more than myself."

I love Tyler's story because it's a perfect example of how someone can start hosting parties, even without a strong base of connections. If you don't have a core group and you've tried everything listed in this chapter to build your own, make like Tyler and find yourself an Erica—someone who already has friends in the area—that you could co-host with.

> [www] See www.party.pro/cohost for my best practices
> in hosting with a partner.

A Note (and Tips) for Readers with Kids

Little humans aren't intentionally excluded from my book. But *The 2-Hour Cocktail Party* was written and tested at a time when I and most of my friends didn't have kids.

Having children at a party often results in the divided attention of your guests. Kids can be a crutch for introverted adults to avoid grown-up interaction. Friends of mine who have kids and host parties recommend getting a sitter to help child-wrangle. They also recommend throwing a parallel kid party in a separate area of the home.

> "Getting a babysitter was a huge help. It's fun for the kids
> and fun for the parents to be able to give their full atten-
> tion to their guests and the purpose of the event."
> —Crystal Zurn

"If we don't have help, my husband and I will be distracted from our party. Without dedicated family or friend assistance, we have to take turns disengaging from our guests to prevent the death and dismemberment of our two active children."

—Caroline Raasch Alquist

"When we hosted a party for couples, my wife and I hired a babysitter for parents who couldn't get one themselves. The kid space was completely separate from the party. Parents only went upstairs to check on their children once or twice throughout the night. It worked great for us because having a babysitter removed a huge barrier to entry for our friends to attend."

—Justin Evans

When your kids get a little older, you may want to include them in your events. Have them welcome guests or help with snacks.

Just make sure they have their own name tags.

☑ CHAPTER CHECKLIST

☐ Make a list of five to ten people who can be in your core group.

☐ Start making a longer list of the great guests that you'll invite. Include neighbors, friends, classmates, and colleagues.

☐ You'll want fifteen total people to come to your party, which means you might need to invite twenty to thirty.

☐ Don't invite important new relationships or critical work contacts yet. Plan for your first party to be a practice run where the stakes are low.

CHAPTER 5

The Magic of
Name Tags

A party without name tags is like a museum without labels for the paintings. You may think that name tags make events cold, bland, formal, or fake. I'm going to convince you otherwise. Watch me.

Name tags make it impossible to forget someone's name.

The Big Benefits

On a practical level, name tags make it nearly impossible for guests to forget each other's names. This reduces potential embarrassment. I'm not great with names myself, so I rely on name tags heavily as a host.

Name tags also boost your guests' confidence because they:

- Reduce social anxiety and make introductions easier.

- Show that this is a safe opportunity to approach strangers.

- Place everyone on equal footing. Even famous celebrities and public figures have to wear them.

The One Where I Forgot Her Name

I know from experience how embarrassing it can be to forget the name of someone who has just introduced themselves. Some years ago, my then-girlfriend and I attended a large corporate event in the SoHo neighborhood of Manhattan. When we arrived, we bumped into a woman who I'd met a few times before. I knew she ran a successful business in New York City with dozens of employees and Fortune 100 customers. But I blanked on her name. It totally slipped my mind.

As I walked up to her, she greeted me warmly and said, "Hello, Nick! It's so nice to see you again." Her arms were open; there she was, smiling, ready to give me a big hug, and I couldn't remember her name. I was mortified. Thinking fast, I introduced her to my girlfriend in the hope that she'd mention her name back. She didn't.

I felt embarrassed and frustrated. Embarrassed because I'd forgotten this woman's name. And frustrated because it would have been so easy for the hosts to avoid this situation just by giving everyone a name tag. I could tell she knew I'd forgotten her name and I potentially missed out on a deeper connection because of it.

Forgetting someone's name is normal and has nothing to do with their level of importance. This CEO had made a huge impression when we previously met, but I just couldn't remember her name. Using name tags ensures this doesn't happen to anyone.

My colleague Michael Alexis shared this advice for when you forget a name and don't have the aid of a name tag:

> "Tackle it head-on. Raise your brow and say something like, 'Can I confess something? I don't remember your name. Will you please remind me?' It's normal to forget a name. It's more awkward to pretend you didn't."

Being sincere in moments like this can actually help people trust you and bring you closer together.

I'm so bad with names that I've written the names of first dates on the inside of my hand to not forget. I was only caught once. (There was no second date.)

The Deeper Purpose of Name Tags

Let's get philosophical for a moment. Why are you interested in hosting parties? Probably because you want to meet new people and bring your friends together. You either are or want to be a "people person." You'd like to make new connections and deepen existing relationships.

Perhaps you're also interested in improving your public speaking. Or you want to get better at facilitating groups for some professional ambition. Maybe you want to find a new job or recruit new clients.

Cocktail parties can do all of this and more. They're places where you, your colleagues, and your friends can meet great new people. It's easier to meet people in an environment that facilitates and supports that goal. Name tags signify that there are no cliques at this party. It's important to show that guests haven't walked into a group of best friends who already know each other. They've walked into a room of potential new connections.

Name tags are a badge guests wear that say they're ready to talk to other people. They're a welcoming and unifying visual signal. Name tags are a humbling feature that tie your party together and put everyone on the same level.

Imagine a charity sports event where everyone is wearing the same color T-shirt. Or a business conference with branded name badges and lanyards. Participants are aligned. At a structured cocktail party, name tags play the same role. When everyone wears a name tag, everyone is on the same team.

PARTY PRO TIP

Name tags are especially helpful when you mix friend groups. Your guests will talk to new people and not stick to their cliques.

Start Using Name Tags at Your First Party

Make name tags part of your hosting strategy from the beginning. If you do this for your first party, you'll build the confidence to keep doing it later. This is especially helpful when you expand your network and start inviting people you don't know so well.

Some hosts object to name tags because they find them too formal. They claim they want to keep the vibe of their party "chill" and believe name tags are incompatible with that. It's a bit odd to use name tags at home, they say. This is an understandable first response.

Hosts—and sometimes guests—frequently resist name tags. This resistance is one of the biggest reasons I'm so vocal about using them. If you are hesitant about using name tags, push through that feeling for your first party. You'll see that it'll be worth it.

Name tags are as much for you as they are for your guests. I helped a newly married couple who had just moved to Texas.

They planned to host their church group using my party for-
mula and invited every member over to their house. At first, the
guests didn't understand the purpose of the name tags. After all,
they already knew the names of everyone. But their hosts didn't.
By agreeing to wear name tags, the guests made it easier for the
hosts. The hosts could meet new people, connect names with
faces, and be present in the conversations. They didn't have to
get distracted trying to memorize a dozen new names.

Practical Matters

When your guests start to arrive, your number one priority is
to warmly welcome them into your home. Give them a hug, a
fist bump, or even a very animated smile. Say that you're happy
they came. Your number two priority is to give them a name
tag. That's how important this step is. If you see people walk-
ing around your party without name tags, pull them aside and
get your naked guest a name tag as soon as possible. Don't let
them move a muscle—except their name-tag-getting muscle.

Write First Names Only

Don't use your guests' surnames. Their first name is faster to
write and easier to read.

Use Large Capital Letters

Your priority is legibility at a distance, not penmanship. Write
names in block letters with a black marker.

Do this: a first name written in big, clear letters is easy to read.

Don't do this: a full name written in cursive with a pen is harder to read.

Make Sure Guests Wear Their Name Tags in Places Where They're Easily Visible

There's not much point in wearing name tags if other guests can't see them. For most people, the best place is the upper chest and lower front shoulder area on their right-hand side. That's the side most of us shake with. It is the easiest place to see a name tag when you meet somebody as your body moves forward to shake hands.

At a recent party, one of my guests didn't want to wear a name tag. She placed it on her pant leg, so it was hidden and inconspicuous. This friend had just started a great new job at the American Museum of Natural History. I was excited for my friends to meet her, especially because the nature of my company's work lends itself to supportive connections among museum workers. But because no one could see her name tag, she didn't look like she belonged at the party.

Eventually I asked her to leave.

Make sure guests place name tags where they are easily visible.

Just kidding. But I did ask her to move her name tag and make it more visible. You can joke about this kind of attention to detail, but it's what turns a good event into a great one.

ASK THE PARTY PROFESSIONAL

Q: What if someone is wearing a silk top or a fancy suit and they don't want to wear a name tag?

A: Quality adhesive name badges remove cleanly and are "dry clean only" friendly. They won't damage the fabric. See the ones I like best at www.party.pro/supplies.

Do Not Write Out Name Tags
Before the Party Begins

Handing out pre-written name tags feels like a conference rather than a cocktail party. And if you pre-write them, your guests can see if there are no-shows. Instead, write out name tags as your guests arrive. It shouldn't take more than five seconds. This way the name tags feel fun and spontaneous. Ask your guest their name if you've forgotten it, how to spell it if you're not certain, and then write their name tag.

Make Sure You Write All the Name Tags

Don't let your guests write their own names. Write the names yourself. Left to their own devices, your guests may use hard-to-read writing. Or worse: dodge their responsibility and not do it at all.

 Do: write first names only, in large capital letters with a black marker.

 Don't: use fancy handwriting or ballpoint pen.

After moving into a new house in Texas, Amy hosted a party with name tags. Unfortunately, she didn't make sure that her guests all wore one. Instead, she left them out on a counter and casually assigned the responsibility to a friend. One guest didn't want to give his real name. He asked the person responsible for name tags to write "Superman" instead. Soon another guest saw that someone was using a joke name and asked for "Batman." Ultimately, half the party's guests sported real names, a quarter gave joke names, and another quarter didn't wear name tags at all. Those who wore them as intended ended up feeling foolish.

Enforce the Wearing of Name Tags

Name tags work best when 100 percent of your guests are on board. Your party is only as strong as the weakest link. If one or two people stop wearing them and new arrivals see the policy is negotiable, the whole system is threatened. Make someone a new tag if they "accidentally" lost it. Be kind but firm. You're creating a great space for new relationships to grow.

The Final Word on Name Tags

As Dale Carnegie, author of *How to Win Friends and Influence People*, says, "A person's name is to him or her the sweetest and most important sound in any language." The easiest way to make that sweet sound happen is to use name tags. Save your guests from embarrassment. Make it easy for everyone to remember names. All it takes is a simple name tag.

☑ CHAPTER CHECKLIST

- [ ] Buy name tags before your party. Have twice as many as you may need. At the time of publishing, I like the Avery brand sized 2 1/3" × 3 3/8" best. Find links to the ones I currently like, and my reviews of others, at www.party.pro/nametags.

- [ ] Write your guests' first names in large capital letters when they arrive. Use a thick black marker.

- [ ] No exceptions: you must use name tags for everyone at your party.

PART 2

Putting the Party Together: The Logistics

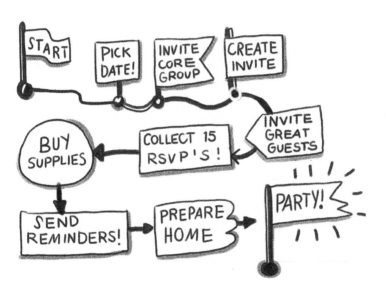

CHAPTER 6

Sending Out the First Invitations

It is time to send the first invitations for your party. This is exciting! Remember that you'll send out your party invites in two separate rounds: first to your core group, and then later to a broader cross section of contacts which are your great guests. We'll deal with that in Chapter 8.

This is not to imply that there is a separation of first- and second-choice people at your party. Everyone mingles together and is equally important. The point is to confirm at least five members of your core group before you invite others.

How to Invite Your Core Group

Choose the communication channel that's right for your relationship. I send casual texts to my friends and maybe a slightly more polite email to colleagues.

Make your invitation messages short and personal. Long party invites feel inauthentic and boilerplate. They're too formal. Err on the side of brevity. Be direct and light.

 Do: individually message each person in your core group.

 Don't: mass message or group text.

I've seen people skip inviting their core group with personal messages. They try to do it on a group text or by clicking to add everyone to a Facebook event. It rarely ends well. Don't skip this step.

Invitation Scripts

Here's the exact wording I've used to invite my core group to my parties. Copy or adapt these scripts for your own use.

> Hey Derek, I'm thinking of hosting a little cocktail party on Wednesday the 8th at 7 p.m. If I do it, would you come? Can I send you some more info?

Why It Works

This message works well because it

- is short;

- is personalized;

- includes an exact date and time;

- gives you wiggle room to change the date and time;

- makes a clear request (Would you come?); and

- makes another ask (Can I send you some more info?). This allows someone who is curious but not yet willing to commit to reply yes.

If they reply with a yes, you'll send them a link to RSVP. You'll create this link in the next chapter after you get five yes replies. For now, just write back and say:

```
Great. I'll make an RSVP page and send you more
info soon.
```

More Formal Core Group Invitation Messages

These are slightly more formal messages that work better in a business setting.

> Hi Sandra. I'm planning to host a cocktail party on Wednesday the 8th at 7 p.m. Are you available then? May I send you some more information about it?

> Hi Geoff. I want to bring some of my friends and colleagues together for a little cocktail party at my home. I'm looking at Wednesday the 8th at 7 p.m. Are you available then? May I send you some more info?

Vulnerable Examples

Sometimes being vulnerable and honest with your core group helps. You can share your desire to be a better host as a more transparent reason why you're hosting a party. A few readers of early drafts of this book who self-identify as introverts told me that they appreciated this method.

> Hi Casey. I'm reading a book about how to bring my friends together and host a cocktail party. I want to throw my first one on Wednesday the 8th at 7 p.m. Would you come? Can I send you some more info?

Rachel, I want to bring some of my favorite people together and am learning how to host a cocktail party. I am inviting friends and work colleagues to my first one. If I have it on Wednesday the 8th at 7 p.m., would you come? May I send you some more information?

Party People in Action: Seth Hanes

Digital Marketing Consultant in New York, New York

Nick: What have you gained by hosting parties?
Seth: The confidence to know that I can continue meeting new people on my own terms. That is an amazing feeling after moving to a new city. I was able to accelerate the process by becoming the person that connected my existing friends to new ones while also developing new relationships.

Nick: Who do you invite to your parties?
Seth: My first cocktail party had ten people show up. It was an absolute blast. The crowd was a mix of new and old friends. It gave me a chance to spend more time with my neighbor and a few coworkers I had recently met.

Nick: What's the biggest challenge or fear you've faced hosting parties?

Seth: My biggest fear about hosting a party with this book was that it would feel too forced and unnatural. The idea of having my friends (some of which already knew each other) wear name tags and do icebreakers felt a little intimidating. But it turned out to make the party smoother for everyone. It allowed all attendees to easily meet and get to know new people that they might not have interacted with otherwise.

Yes or No: Confirming the Date

Once you've messaged your core group with a proposed date and time for your party, you'll start to receive responses of yes, no, or maybe, or if you're me, "For the last time, we are a sushi supply store—not your friend."

Your goal is to receive five yes confirmations.

 PARTY PRO TIP

For the purposes of counting here, consider any maybe response as a no.

When you get five yes replies, continue to the next chapter to build your event page and collect RSVPs.

ASK THE PARTY PROFESSIONAL

Q: How long should I wait for responses from my core group?

A: One or two days. If you haven't heard back, and if you don't yet have five yes responses, message them again. I send a short note like this:

> Hi! Any thoughts on that date for my party?

If you still don't hear back, assume they are a no.

Trying Another Date

If your first date and time doesn't receive enough yes confirmations, don't be discouraged or take it personally. Just try again with a new date for your party, perhaps one week later or on another day of the week.

> Hi again. I'm trying a new date for my cocktail party. Would Tuesday, June 14, at 7 p.m. work?

Through trying a few different days of the week and times, you should be able to get at least five people to commit to attending. Don't worry if you think you will bother your friends with multiple requests. People appreciate being included and invited. Besides, you're texting them about a party. You're planning a fun event to meet new people, not asking them to help you move. It really is OK to ask.

☑ CHAPTER CHECKLIST

☐ It's time to send your first invitations. Woohoo!

☐ Message each person in your core group individually to invite them to your party.

☐ Write back to each person who said yes or maybe, to tell them that you'll send more information soon.

☐ When you get five yes replies, congratulations: you're hosting a party! Move on to the next chapter to build your event page and start collecting RSVPs.

☐ If you can't get five yes replies after two days of trying, change the date of your party, and try again.

CHAPTER 7

Setting Up the Event Page

Now that you've received five yes responses from your core group, you're ready to make it official and collect their RSVPs. The best way to do this is to create a simple online event page for your party. This helps build excitement, set expectations, and entice your great guests to RSVP when you invite them in the next chapter.

Pick Your Platform

When I first started to host my cocktail parties, I used Facebook to create and share my events with friends. It was a quick and simple way to lock in RSVPs and communicate with guests.

But often my friends would miss my invitations or important reminder messages. Some of them didn't use social media. I began experimenting with other platforms like Eventbrite and Paperless Post. Those platforms allowed me to email reminders to my guests, which dramatically improved attendance. I could also present a more professional image while still having fun.

> [www] See the actual event pages I've used for my parties at www.party.pro/events1.

At the time of publishing, these are four platforms I recommend:

	Good	Bad
Mixily	• Super simple setup • No ads, no spam • Works great on mobile • Easy to download a CSV of all RSVPs for emailing	• Less custom and fancy designs
Facebook	• Easiest to set up and RSVP • Easy to share reminders • Guests can connect with each other	• Unless they regularly use Facebook, guests might not see your event and reminder messages • Some people don't use Facebook or are not connected to you

Paperless Post	• Variety of fun party templates • New free Flyer product is fast and easy • Good mobile app	• Sometimes invitations and messages go to spam • Certain features require a paid account
Evite	• Well-known, established brand for events • Good for families. Allows RSVPs with number of adults, children	• Tons of advertisements on your RSVP page • Sometimes invitations and messages go to spam

If you're in a rush, try Paperless Post Flyer. My personal favorite and the one I recommend to my friends is Mixily. Use the one you feel will work best for your needs. The steps are generally the same whatever platform you choose.

www Event platforms and features can change. For an updated list of the services I recommend, including best practices for each, visit www.party.pro/platforms.

Create the Event Page

Title Your Event

For your first party, title it "Cocktails and Icebreakers Party." This type of title cements the expectation that there'll be structure to the gathering. When you call it a "Cocktails and Icebreakers Party," your guests won't be surprised when you lead icebreakers. They agree to participate, too, when they RSVP. There's absolutely no room for confusion.

You can build on that basic title to make your party more relevant to your guests. Titles like "Cocktails and Icebreakers with St. Louis's Best" or "Cocktails and Icebreakers to Celebrate Spring" work well.

Write the Event Description

The event description furthers your guests' excitement. It includes information to let them know what they're signing up for.

Here's a sample event description I've used for my events:

> I'm hosting a cocktail party!
>
> Super casual, meet new friends, see old ones, and have a drink on me.
>
> I'll have name tags, a few bottles of wine, whiskey, vodka, and tons of sparkling water. There'll be chips or light snacks but no formal dinner.
>
> My apartment is on the top floor of a very old building in Greenwich Village. Shoes off inside, please.

It makes me happy to introduce great people and new friends. My favorite part of the night is when we do icebreakers. Have you ever been at a party and wished you could have met even more new, fun, interesting people? Name tags and ice-breakers make it easy to do that. Hope to see you soon!

Set Guests' Expectations

Since most other parties don't use icebreakers and name tags, you should let guests know about them in advance by mentioning them in the event title and description. Then anyone who RSVPs to your party is agreeing to participate at your party with these structural elements. They're giving you permission to host and run a great event. They know they're coming to a party with a purpose.

 Do: mention there will be name tags and icebreakers in your event description.

 Don't: decide to leave them out, trying to be a "cool" or "easygoing" host.

Quick icebreakers where everyone introduces themselves are an essential component of every party I host. Even if you think they sound corny now, I promise that they will work wonders for your gathering. You will learn everything you need to feel confident about icebreakers in Chapter 12, including scripts for how to do them and which ones are my favorites.

A few people I've advised either forgot to mention these details or didn't think it was a necessary component. Cesar, a locksmith shop owner in Atlanta, didn't give his guests a heads-up in his event description about doing icebreakers at his first party. When he started to introduce everyone, his guests were unprepared and a bit confused about what he was asking them to do. This mismatch in expectations caused him a lot of unnecessary anxiety.

Compare that to his second party:

> "I nearly copied your event description from the book this time. It helped explain the 'why' of doing icebreakers to meet new people. Nobody resisted them. I was surprised how well they worked to help get new people talking."

Choose a Fun Featured Image

You can stylize your event page with a graphic or theme on most platforms. Choose something bold that conveys a sense of fun and expresses your personality.

Think of your event page like an online dating profile. The photo is the first thing people will see. If you don't include a good photo, you will get less matches—the equivalent to less RSVPs.

[www] To see featured images I've used for my parties,
visit www.party.pro/images1. They include
beaches, vintage parties, and hip museums.

An eye-catching image that creates excitement or makes someone smile is best. Avoid using something boring and generic. For bonus points, add a fun picture of yourself in the header or towards the end of the event description. This makes the event page feel more personal.

Choose the Right Display and Privacy Settings

Enable the setting on your event platform to show guest names who have RSVP'd. Some platforms allow your guests to indicate if they will bring a plus-one. This is an easy way for new hosts to get more RSVPs.

On Mixily, enabling these options looks like this:

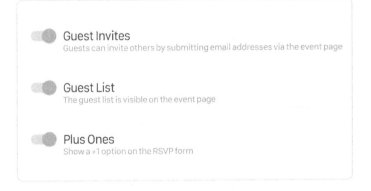

Guest Invites
Guests can invite others by submitting email addresses via the event page

Guest List
The guest list is visible on the event page

Plus Ones
Show a +1 option on the RSVP form

Be mindful of privacy settings too. By default, most platforms will only show your event to those you invite or send the link to. Don't list your party as public and open to anyone on the internet.

Test the RSVP Link

Fill out the rest of the details for your party, including the date, time, and location. When you're finished, save and publish your new event.

Send the link to your party page to yourself via email and text message. Click on the link. Make sure it looks good from the perspective of a guest. Confirm that all the details are correct.

 PARTY PRO TIP

Sign up and RSVP for your own party as a final confirmation. Use a real email address to check the messages your guests will receive.

Stack the Deck

Now that your party page is complete, the crucial next step is to message each person in your core group who said yes. Ask them to RSVP on the event page you just published.

Because you selected the option to make the guest list visible, it will begin to list the names of everyone who has RSVP'd. This will "stack the deck" for your party.

Collecting RSVPs drives better attendance by:

- Reaffirming each person's commitment to attend.

- Getting them to make a social contract by announcing to others on the event page that they plan to attend.

- Building social proof for the party by adding their name to the guest list.

Building social proof[1] is important. A party with nobody listed as attending doesn't look like a very exciting event. When you reach out to invite some of your great guests in the next chapter, they'll see that several people are already attending. That makes the party you're about to host look much more appealing than an empty room.

1   The term "social proof" was coined by Robert Cialdini in his book *Influence*. He said that "we view a behavior as more correct in a given situation to the degree that we see others performing it." I'm using it here like FOMO, or Fear of Missing Out: when someone sees that your party has a bunch of RSVPs, they are more likely to RSVP themselves.

Ask Your Core Group to RSVP

Follow up with each person in your core group now. I reply to their last message like this:

> This will be fun. Here is the event info page I just made. Will you do me a favor and click to RSVP? [EVENT LINK HERE]

Here's a transcript showing that message in context:

> **Me**: Hey Derek, I'm thinking of hosting a little cocktail party on Wednesday the 8th at 7 p.m. If I do it, could you come? Can I send you more info?
>
> **Derek**: Yes, I'm free then. Send me the info.
>
> **Me**: Great. I'll make an RSVP page and send you more info soon.

[I brew a pot of tea and make the event page.]

> **Me**: This will be fun. Here is the event info page that I just made. Will you do me a favor and click to RSVP? [EVENT LINK HERE]

ASK THE PARTY PROFESSIONAL

Q: Should I follow up with confirmed "yes" guests to remind them to RSVP on the event page?

A: Yes. You really want to fill up your list of RSVPs. It might sound annoying, but you should always follow up with confirmed "yes" guests who haven't yet RSVP'd. It is so important to have a full RSVP list for the success of your party. Message the person via text or email and say:

Small reminder: Would you please RSVP here real quick? Only takes a minute and helps me with getting a head count [EVENT LINK HERE]

Beware of Bad Ratios

I'm sure you've seen event pages where forty-seven people were invited but only two people are confirmed as attending. This is a bad party ratio. It suggests the host went with the spray-and-pray approach to invitations. They sent untargeted mass invites in the hope that a few random people will show up.

GOING   INTERESTED   INVITED

When I get invited to an event like this, I'm less likely to RSVP and much less likely to attend. My invitation doesn't feel special—it feels like spam. I worry that I'll be one of only a few people who show up.

 Do: make each of your guests feel special by personally inviting them to your party before you send them the link to RSVP.

 Don't: spam your party invitations. Never send the link to RSVP before checking if someone is interested or available.

Acquaintances are always nervous about being the first to say yes to something. It requires a lot of courage. There's a high level of friction. You'll avoid this when you first get your core group to add their names on your event page. Their RSVPs will give you momentum (it's like a domino effect!) and build social proof for your party.

☑ CHAPTER CHECKLIST

☐ Choose an online platform and create a new event to collect RSVPs for your party.

☐ Title your party "Cocktails and Icebreakers."

☐ Write a description that sets expectations. Mention the name tags and icebreakers.

☐ Add a fun image or theme.

☐ Change any settings for your event, like making the guest list visible and allowing people to bring a plus-one.

☐ Test sending the link to your event page to yourself. Click to RSVP and confirm that everything works.

☐ Send that link to each person in your core group who will come to your party. Have them RSVP before you start to invite your great guests in the next chapter.

☐ Nice job so far! Feel confident knowing you're doing good work to guarantee that your party will be a success.

CHAPTER 8

Inviting Your Great Guests

Now your party is official. Your event page is live and your core group has RSVP'd. It's time to start inviting more people and fill up your guest list. This will be fun!

Three Steps for Inviting Great Guests

You'll invite your list of great guests with a similar formula as before with your core group. But now you'll add a bit more information to your first message.

1. Invite the person to your event: use a personalized message.

2. **If they respond yes or maybe:** reply with the event page link and ask them to RSVP. Only send a link to your event page if they've responded yes or maybe.

3. **If they respond no:** ask if you can invite them the next time you host an event. If they say yes, make your next party list and add them to it. I use a simple spreadsheet to help track this.[1]

The Anatomy of a Great Guest Invitation

The invitation to a great guest is a longer message than what you sent to someone in your core group. It assumes you don't know the person as well. They might need more context to understand what you're doing or what your intentions are.

Here's exactly what I send via email to invite a great guest:

Hi Mark,

I'm getting some friends and colleagues together for a little cocktail party. Do you want to come?

It'll be on Wednesday, June 8, from 7 to 9 p.m.

---

1   For managing my list of contacts, including how I sort and what I track, see my notes at www.party.pro/spreadsheet.

I'm hosting it at my apartment at 1000 5th Avenue,
NY NY 10028.

I'd love to introduce you to a few people I think
you'd hit it off with. I will have name tags
and icebreakers because I'm trying to be a good
host, haha.

Are you free then? Or can I send you some more
info?

—Nick

A message like this sets the expectation that there will be
name tags and icebreakers. I purposefully include "haha" to
imply that the mood will be lighthearted. Without it, the
message could come across as more formal or formulaic.

The line at the end, "Or can I send you some more info?" again
gives the recipient the chance to say yes when they're not yet
ready to commit.

For a shorter and more informal text message version of this,
I send:

Cesar! I'm hosting a little cocktail party on
Wed, June 8, from 7 to 9p with name tags and

icebreakers (haha). Would love to introduce you to a few friends and colleagues. Are you free then? Or can I send you more info?

Party People in Action: Luke Murray

Family Medicine Doctor in Louisville, Kentucky

Nick: Why did you decide to start hosting parties?

Luke: I moved to a small town and was working twelve-hour days. I wanted a way to develop meaningful relationships outside of work. I couldn't do that by just going out to dinner with random people I met at the hospital. So, I started hosting parties. They make it easy for me to invite people I meet and want to hang out with again.

Nick: Who do you invite to your parties?

Luke: I invite anyone I meet that I like. There are a lot of doctors and medical students. I'm also learning to fly a plane, so I invited my flight instructor. I met someone in a shoe store who was super smart and knowledgeable about shoes and hip-hop—he got an invite too.

Nick: What have you gained by hosting parties?

Luke: Connections and legitimate friendships in a town where I didn't know many people. And the confidence

> to host more parties and make more connections. Using this framework to host has boosted my progress by more than a year. It would have taken me a dozen parties to figure this out on my own.

It's OK to Be Vulnerable

As with your core group, don't be afraid to show vulnerability when you send out messages to great guests about your party. You can share that you're learning to host using an introduction sentence like this:

> Hi Nina, I'm reading a book on how to host cocktail parties and bring people together. Some friends and work colleagues are coming to my first one on Wednesday the 8th at 7 p.m.

I advised one anxious host to admit that they had never thrown a cocktail party before. They mentioned in their invitation that they're hosting an event as part of a challenge in reading this book and acknowledged it would mean a lot if their colleague came.

> Hey Wayne, I'm learning how to host a fun cocktail party as part of a challenge. I'm a bit nervous

to do my first one and could really use a friendly
face there! Haha. My first one is on Wednesday the
8th at 7 p.m.

That honesty worked in the new host's favor. It was endearing
to the person receiving the invite. And it kept the host more
relaxed since they didn't have to pretend otherwise.

Show vulnerability by telling your guests that you're new to hosting.
They will appreciate your honesty and won't expect you to be an expert.

ASK THE PARTY PROFESSIONAL

Q: Should I follow up with great guests who don't reply
to the invite? How long do you give them to reply?

A: Sure. If you haven't heard back in three days, send a
friendly message like this:

> Hi again! No reply needed if you're busy, but I
> wanted to make sure you saw this. Can I send you
> the party link for more info? It is going to be
> fun.

Plus-Ones and Significant Others

When you invite someone to your party, they might ask if they can bring a guest, a significant other, or a plus-one. If you haven't yet reached your goal of fifteen yes RSVPs, then tell them yes. Having someone else join your party is great. It is usually "the more the merrier" for first-time hosts when your goal is simply to manage a crowd and practice logistics of this formula.

 PARTY PRO TIP
Ask their plus-one to RSVP on your event page.
It will set their expectations and allow you to
include them in your reminder messages.

As you advance in your hosting skills, you may want to curate your guest list more carefully. Then you might not want plus-ones or significant others. When someone brings a date to the party, they almost always spend less time meeting new people.

If I was curating a specific group of people, or if I was a new host and I didn't want any more guests at my party, I'd say this:

```
I wish I could let you bring them! But my party
is already full with the maximum number that
I'm comfortable hosting. Part of the purpose of
this party is for me to practice being a better
host. More people makes it harder to manage. Is
that OK?
```

I like adding the "Is that OK?" at the end as a way to get their buy-in.

Next Steps

Start inviting your great guests now. Then answer their responses.

Yes Reply

```
Super. This'll be fun. Here's the info page:
[EVENT LINK HERE]
Will you do me a favor and RSVP there so I can get
a head count?
```

Maybe Reply

```
OK! Here is the info page:
[EVENT LINK HERE]
Please RSVP there if you can make it.
```

No Reply

```
Sorry to miss you. And thanks for writing back.
Can I invite you to the next one?
```

Try to get fifteen people to RSVP. It may take a few days for some to reply. That's normal. It is all part of having a long runway leading up to your party date. If it takes more than one week for you to get fifteen RSVPs, go back to Chapter 4. Review the sections "Creating a Core Group When You Don't Have One" and "How to Grow Your Guest List" for ideas about how to invite more people.

Now is a courteous time to tell your neighbors that you'll be hosting a small gathering. Give them a heads up that you're expecting visitors and from what times.

Soon your party will start to fill up with confirmations. Great job! In the coming days, you will send three reminder messages, buy a few supplies, prepare your space, then host your party. Things are coming together. You're putting in the effort to guarantee that your guests will enjoy the party. At the end, you'll be proud of all that you've accomplished. Hosting parties is a life skill that you're building.

☑ CHAPTER CHECKLIST

☐ Send each of your great guests a personalized invitation with information about your party. Do not mass add people to a Facebook Event, spam out an email, or group text.

☐ If they say yes or maybe, send them the event link you created. Have them RSVP.

☐ If they say no, ask if you can invite them to your next party. Add them to a list of people to invite to your next party.

☐ Collect fifteen yes RSVPs on your event page. Do this within ten days before your party.

☐ If it is ten days or less before your party and you do not yet have fifteen confirmed RSVPs, return to Chapter 4 for ideas of more people to invite.

CHAPTER 9

Sending Out Reminders

You've sent your invitations and collected RSVPs. Next, you'll send a series of pre-party messages that show you've put effort into the planning. These reminders generate excitement, keep your event top of mind, and ensure high attendance. When you use these, you'll stand out in a culture that thrives on the image of people who are too cool to care.

Less Ghosting, More Hosting

Unless you're hosting a wedding or the Met Gala, no-shows are an inevitable part of life for event organizers. People will tell you they are coming to your party and then never show up.

Don't take it personally. People are busy. No-shows happen for a variety of reasons such as work, family, or social emergencies. Or perhaps someone just decided that going home to relax was a better use of their evening.

Your job is to promote your event to guests in a way that generates excitement. From the moment you create your invite until the day of your party, keep your party top of mind. Reminders persuade your invitees that your event is special. When you use these, you'll set yourself apart before the party even starts.

The Three Reminder Messages

Send this sequence of reminder messages to your guests. I create calendar notes for myself because I've found that forgetting to send even one can drop attendance. You'll find the reasoning for each of these plus examples in the pages ahead.

1. **Seven days before:** send out a short reminder that includes logistical info plus a fun, lighthearted image attachment.

2. **Three days before:** this is my favorite. Send another reminder which includes a brief biographical note about many of your guests. I call these your guest bios. This message takes the most time to create but has the potential to be the single greatest hook to ensure excitement and solid attendance.

3. **Morning of the party:** send a final reminder. Include any logistical information—like your address and phone number—clearly up top.

How to Send Reminders

Use email or the messaging tools built into your event platform to send your reminders. Mass messages are bad for invitations, but they're great for communicating with people who have already RSVP'd. They've signed up to get them!

If you're using email, blind carbon copy (BCC) everybody who has said yes or maybe to your RSVP. Send the email to yourself and include all of your guests in the BCC field. You'll respect their privacy and email addresses when you use BCC instead of carbon copy (CC). You'll also save your guests from unintended reply-all cancellation notes or questions.

Perhaps you worry that you're overcommunicating with your guests. This is a totally normal concern but unnecessary. In all my time as a host, no one has ever told me that they heard from me too many times in the lead-up to the party. Instead, what I've gotten is a consistently high proportion of RSVPs actually showing up to my party.[1]

You want your event to be a success. You want people to enjoy themselves. Your enthusiasm is genuine. Share it authentically and you will never annoy people. Fun reminders require nothing of recipients beyond a quick read. Far from being annoying, they can brighten the days of your guest list and add to their anticipation of your party.

Seven Days Before

The first reminder is a short note that tells your guests you're excited about the party and looking forward to seeing them. Send this message to people who have RSVP'd as well as to those who you haven't heard back from. It's a subtle calendar reminder and a hint to RSVP for those who haven't done so yet.

---

1   A recent party had nineteen RSVPs, of which eighteen attended. That's high even for me. Based on a back-of-the-envelope calculation, I'd estimate the average attendance rate for my parties is 85 percent.

Subject: Party next week

Hey everyone, ONE WEEK AWAY!

The party is next week on Wednesday, June 8, 2022, from 7-9 p.m. It is shaping up to be lots of fun. Looking forward to seeing you all.

As a reminder, here is the page you RSVP'd on: [EVENT LINK HERE]

I like to attach a funny GIF, meme, or group photo from one of my previous parties. This keeps the reminder message fun.

Three Days Before

Prepare to step up your reminder game. Just when people are most likely to develop potential last-minute scheduling conflicts, you send an irresistible reminder using guest bios to ramp up anticipation and commitment.

Guest Bios

Guest bios make it easy for your guests to start conversations and create new connections. They also make people feel special, valued, and excited to attend your party. Guest bios are a guaranteed part of my formula for giving you better attendance and a better party.

A guest bio is a short summary about someone. It could include professional or personal information—or both. But I'm not asking you to write full biographies of your guests just for a cocktail party. Keep it simple and light.

Sample Guest Bios

Here are real bios I've sent out in a reminder message.

A few of the guests at this party will include:

Nick Gray (that's me) is the founder of Museum Hack. My favorite places in New York City are the Met Museum and Washington Square Park.

Stefen Ramirez is the owner of 29b Teahouse in the East Village and Tea Dealers. Ask him about matcha!

Atalanta Xanthe is an artist-in-residence at the New York Academy of Art. I met her a few months ago and liked her work so much that I've invited her tonight.

Seonaid Beckwith runs a website about grammar for English learners. She is Scottish and has been living in London since 2004. I met her via my friend Ramit.

Raf Ignacio is the host of my favorite Filipino food tour in NYC.

Carly Straughan is a business solutions engineer at Gateway Ticketing Systems. She loves theme parks, museums, water parks, and zoos.

Many people have told me they particularly enjoy receiving and reading these guest bios. Here's one testimonial about them:

> "I was taking a chance going to your party where the only person I knew was you. We had just met the previous day during a meeting at my office. The guest bios you sent for your party made me feel like I knew a few other people and increased my enthusiasm for getting to know you and the other guests better. It also fueled my competitive nature to deepen our relationship so I might be invited back and featured in one of the guest bios."

How to Write Your Guest Bios

Writing good guest bios can take twenty minutes or less. Mine usually take me about fifteen. Don't put unnecessary pressure on yourself. These are short, fun notes, not someone's entire life history. They don't all have to be the same length, and you don't have to include every single person.

Do: make the guest bios brief, lively, and informal.

 Don't: make it sound like a resume or a Forbes "30 Under 30" list.

Imagine one of your guests is named Rob Simon. You've known Rob for a year. He works as a copywriter and practices yoga for two hours a day. Rob rides a scooter and recently rescued a dog. He's originally from England and he drinks a lot of herbal tea.

A perfectly fine guest bio for Rob would be:

> **Rob Simon** works as a copywriter. He rides a scooter and recently rescued a dog. Ask him about yoga or herbal tea!

That is simple and fun. It calls out some of his unique attributes in a brief sentence. And hopefully it gives people a reference point to strike up a conversation or ask a question when they meet Rob at your party.

Who Gets a Guest Bio?

Include bios for at least half of your group or eight of your guests, whichever is larger. Err on the side of including more people rather than less. Start with your core group and add other guests who you know well or are excited about.

You don't have to write a guest bio for everyone, and you don't have to feel bad about leaving anyone out. I always say that these bios are only *some* of the attendees. To make sure people understand this, I add a teaser at the end. For example: "plus a few more guests" or "and many more."

Some hosts worry about not including everyone in the guest bios and being fair to all their guests. Include everyone if you want. But know that everyone who shows up will participate in icebreakers. Everyone will wear a name tag and meet whomever they like. The guest bios are just a teaser.

ASK THE PARTY PROFESSIONAL

Q: Do you ask your guests for permission or what they want listed in their guest bio?

A: No, I don't. That would take too much work. I don't mind if I make a mistake. This is a fun cocktail party, not a Nobel Prize announcement. Because I never include sensitive information about someone that couldn't be found on their resume or social media, I feel that respects the privacy of my guests. Plus, I only share the guest bios via email or private message to other party attendees. I've never gotten a complaint.

Example Message

Include all the logistical details for your party, your contact information, and your guest bios. Here's a message I've sent that you can modify:

Subject: Party info ⚡ for Wednesday

Look at this great group of people!

A few friends who are coming to my Cocktails and Icebreakers party are listed below.

Date: Wednesday, June 8, 2022

Time: 7:00-9:00 p.m.

Location: my apartment at
1000 5th Avenue, NY NY 10028
** shoes off inside, so wear nice socks if you want

More info: the event page where you RSVP'd is here
[EVENT LINK HERE]

My phone number is +1-212-555-5555 -- Nick

✎ **Guest bios for Wednesday night**

Rob Simon works as a copywriter. He rides a scooter and recently rescued a dog…

[additional guest bios here]

…plus a few more great people!

One of the reasons I'm hosting this party is to introduce my friends and colleagues. (The other is to have an excuse to wear my new red socks.) Perhaps these fun facts will inspire you to strike up a new conversation.

See you soon

—Nick

P.S. Congrats on getting to the end of this very long email 😄

Why It Works

This message works well because it

- is clear and direct;

- is easy to read;

- puts the most important logistical information up top;

- uses your guest bios to generate excitement;

- briefly explains the "why" behind guest bios at the end; and

- has a few elements of personalization.

Keep this reminder message fast and fun. You'll make it easy to read when you use short sentences, line breaks, and bold sections.

Morning of the Party

Send one final message to your guests on the morning of your party. Copy the last message you sent three days before your party to use as a template. Then update the subject line and add a fresh introduction to express your excitement.

Use this message to inform guests of any important details—for example, directions to your home or any special instructions. Maybe your house is at the end of a cul-de-sac and you've tied a big red balloon to the mailbox. Add that information to this message.

PARTY PRO TIP

Provide guests with your phone number in case they need to contact you with last-minute questions or directions.

But it's not just about details. This final message is particularly aimed at any invitees who might be thinking about backing out or who might have even forgotten about your event. It's your final chance to ensure a strong turnout. Keep it fun and include the guest bios again for those who didn't read them in the last message.

Example Message

```
Subject: Party TONIGHT! ☆


Wow. Great people are coming.
I've got some liquor, wine, and lots of seltzer.
Plus a few salty snacks.
I'm pretty sure that's all we need 😄


Time: 7:00-9:00 p.m.
Location: my apartment at
1000 5th Avenue, NY NY 10028
** buzz #5 outside, then buzz #5 again
** shoes off inside, so wear nice socks if you want
```

More info: the event page where you RSVP'd is here
[EVENT LINK HERE]

My phone number is +1-212-555-5555 -- Nick

✎ **Guest bios, people you'll meet tonight**
Rob Simon works as a copywriter. He rides a scooter
and recently rescued a dog…
[additional guest bios here]
…plus a few more fun folks.

See you tonight!

—Nick

For a less casual introduction that could be used for a profes-
sional event, I send this:

Subject: Cocktail party tonight

I am excited for tonight. We have such a great
group of people attending. Looking forward to
introducing everyone and seeing you all soon. I've
got drinks, name tags, and icebreakers ready.

Invitation continues as prior example, including time,
address, my contact information, and guest bios.

Your final reminder should show your guests that you're excited for the party. Give them tongue-in-cheek reasons why they should be excited too. "Great cocktails, amazing people, and free high fives," for example. I include a few emojis in my reminders, but if that's not your style, delete them. You could also attach a fun picture of yourself, a family-friendly meme, or one of your favorite GIFs.

ASK THE PARTY PROFESSIONAL

Q: How do I answer the guest who asks, "Is there anything I can bring?"

A: I never ask guests to bring anything because I want to make it as easy as possible for people to attend. But if they offer, I say:

```
Thank you so much for offering. It is totally
not necessary to bring anything. But if you're
feeling inspired: a bottle of something you'd
like to drink would be great.
```

Jason's Story: Better Ratios with Better Messaging

Jason is a former colleague. He hosts a monthly meetup for freelancers in Atlanta, Georgia.

Before he started using the reminder messages in this chapter, Jason suffered from low turnouts at his events. Low turnout is an especially common problem for free public meetups. Jason reported an average turnout of 30 percent. Typically, sixty people RSVP'd and only twenty showed up.

I shared with Jason the importance of guest bios in his pre-event messaging. I explained that these messages demonstrate the host is putting work into their event and help keep it top of mind. I also mentioned that guest bios pique people's interest, making them curious about other guests and excited to meet them in person.

Jason took my advice to heart and began to make guest bios a part of his event planning process. As soon as he did, he saw his attendance rate grow from 30 to 50 percent. That's a big leap. And all it took was one simple addition: guest bios.

Don't Be Afraid to Self-Promote

Trevor, an executive for a software startup, told me that he feels uncomfortable hyping up his parties. He feels like he doesn't sound like himself when he uses these reminder messages. In fact, he says it's hard enough for him to send initial invitations, let alone reminders that keep his guests' excitement levels high.

It's normal to feel shy about promoting your party, especially if it's your first one or you're inviting people you don't know that well. Nobody wants to bother their guests.

But don't worry. You can modify these reminder messages to make them fit your voice. With practice, you'll get over this nervousness. After years of hosting, I've become a party hype machine.

For one of my first cocktail parties, I told people I'd serve them the best cocktails they had ever tried. "These drinks will knock your socks off," I said. "I can't wait for you to come over tonight. It's going to be incredible."

Guess what! All I had at that party was a bottle of whiskey, some seltzer, and a little bottle of bitters. And guess what else! No one complained. No one mentioned that I hadn't provided the best cocktails they'd ever tried. My promotion of the party was exciting. Guests found the hype funny and were persuaded to attend. Once they were at my apartment and chatting with new friends, they enjoyed themselves. They weren't bothered about the quality of the free cocktails I provided. It will be the same at your party.

Self-promotion is only a problem if you don't have your guests' best interests at heart. When you're genuinely committed to hosting a great event and bringing people together, you should promote the heck out of it. Nobody will complain.

Make your guests believe that your party will be great, and it will be.

☑ CHAPTER CHECKLIST

☐ Start writing a few guest bios for people in your core group now. Save these in an email draft.

☐ Set calendar reminders for yourself to message your guests seven days before your party, three days before your party, and the morning of the party.

☐ Seven days before your party, send your first reminder message. Attach a fun image to keep the tone light.

☐ Four days before your party, finish writing guest bios for at least half of your guest list or eight people (whichever is higher). Use these to create your next reminder message.

☐ Three days before your party, send the reminder message with all of your guest bios. Also include the date, time, and location of your party.

☐ On the morning of your party, send the last reminder to your guests. Include the time, location, your phone number, and all of your guest bios again.

☐ Great job! You're definitely not too cool to care. In fact, you're putting in the effort to create connections and guarantee great attendance. Your guests will be impressed.

CHAPTER 10

Pre-Party Preparations

While preparing for one of the first big cocktail parties I hosted at my apartment in Brooklyn, I made one of the worst party hosting mistakes ever.

A lot of friends had RSVP'd, and I spent much of the afternoon frantically cleaning. I prepared delicious food, which took way longer than I anticipated. I spent time rearranging furniture and decorating with banners and balloons. All of this was stressful and left me freaking out as the time of the party approached.

The party was due to start at 7:00 p.m. At 6:45, I was still wearing grubby gym clothes. I hadn't even showered. And it didn't occur to me that my first guests might arrive a few minutes early.

Unfortunately, that's exactly what happened. I jumped in the shower and the next thing I knew, the doorbell rang. I didn't want to leave one of my guests standing on my doorstep. So, I jumped back out of the shower. I opened the door to my new friend, Nora, as I stood there dripping wet and dressed in just a towel.

This really happened to me.

I was mortified. My party had barely started, and I was already behind. And I was naked. To my early guest, it looked as though I didn't have my act together. Instead of presenting the image of a ready host, I presented the exact opposite. My apartment looked great, but I was a mess.

Don't let this happen to you.

What did I get wrong? Lots. For starters, I was trying to live up to the image of a perfect host. I spent too much time preparing food and decorations that my guests truly didn't care about. I forgot that they were there for me, for their friends and colleagues, and to meet new people. That was enough.

I've learned to simplify since then. When I host parties now, I clean the day before, I take faster showers, and I focus on what's most important instead of the trivial things.

Sweat the Right Stuff

It's inevitable that you'll experience some anxiety when you decide to host. Your palms may get sweaty. You'll second-guess your core group, and you'll check and recheck your event page a dozen times for typos. On the day of the party, you might watch the clock, wondering if anyone will show.

This is a good thing. You're anxious because you care.

Don't stop caring. Just care about the *right* things and prepare in advance.

Many who choose to host a party become so preoccupied with what food or drinks they should serve that they decide parties are a nightmare. They swear off hosting forever and say they'll never do it again.

When your party is over, I don't want you to look back and wonder if people liked the food. I want you to look back and think, *Wow. That was fun and easy. Everyone really hit it off. I want to host again.*

A Short List of Essential Supplies

Keep your shopping list to a minimum. Know just what you need and purchase it a week or more in advance. Here are a few items I consider essential:

- name tags

- alcohol and mixers

- disposable cups

- simple snacks

- harmonica (I'll explain later)

PARTY SHOPPING LIST FOR FIFTEEN PEOPLE

Download a printable version of this checklist at www.party.pro/print.

Alcohol

- 750 mL bottles of both whiskey and vodka, or other liquor (tequila!)
- Two bottles each of red and white wine

Mixers

- 4 L of sparkling water or twenty-four cans
- 1 L of cranberry or orange juice
- 1 L each of diet and regular soda

Snacks

- Baby carrots: 1 lb. (450 g)
- Hummus: 8 or 12 oz. (300 g)
- Guacamole: 1 lb. (450 g)
- Chips: two 12–15 oz. bags (370 g)
- Nuts, salted: 16 oz. (450 g)
- Cheese plate: 2 lbs. (900 g) (optional)
- Grapes: 2 lbs. (900 g)

Supplies

- Thirty name tags and four black Sharpie markers
- Disposable cups
- 5 lbs. of ice
- Paper towels or other cleaning supplies for drink spills
- Lightly scented candle for bathroom

Name Tags

You know how vital name tags are to the success of your party. Use any brand and style you prefer. What's most important is that the name tags you use have a large blank white space where you can write the guest's name.

Stickers marketed and sold as name tags will be designed not to damage people's clothing. They are easy to write on and remove. Be careful of trying to use multipurpose stickers as name tags. On one occasion, I bought shipping labels for an event because they were less expensive. They didn't stick properly to clothing and started to curl and fall off after thirty minutes.

Alongside name tags, I recommend purchasing a Sharpie or another thick, black marker to write your guests' names with. This will make the names easy to read. Whiteboard markers can work well too. Avoid the mistake of buying name tags and writing names in ballpoint pen or, even worse, pencil. Names written in pen or pencil are hard to read, especially from a distance.

(www) To see a ranked list of my current favorite name tags that you can order online, visit www.party. pro/nametags.

If you only take one thing from this book, make it a commitment to purchasing and using name tags at your party. They are the single biggest trick for facilitating new conversations and making people feel welcome.

Alcohol and Mixers

Many new hosts get stressed when they think about serving drinks. They don't know how to make cocktails. They can't imagine hosting a cocktail party, so they never do it. They miss the opportunity of using this effective event format.

Thankfully, that won't happen to you. You know that a good gathering is not about the quality of the cocktails. The drinks don't really matter. What matters is that your guests will meet interesting people and have a few new conversations. This is why you're hosting a party: to create connections, build relationships, and bring people together.

Trust me—your guests will not be expecting amazing cocktails unless you're a trained mixologist. You're hosting an event to welcome people into your home, not as an opportunity for you to play bartender. So keep the drinks simple. Your bar area will be self-serve. You'll provide a variety of drink options in the easiest possible way.

Here's my essential list of alcohol and mixers to have available:

- **Liquor:** 750 mL each of whiskey and vodka, or another popular liquor such as bourbon, rum, or tequila. I avoid the cheapest options and typically buy brands such as Svedka for vodka, Jack Daniel's for whiskey, Maker's Mark for bourbon, etc. Get whatever fits your budget.

 PARTY PRO TIP

As long as the liquor you buy is in a glass bottle and not plastic, it'll do fine for an adult party.

- Wine: Two bottles each of white and red wine, preferably screw-top for simplicity.[1] Rosé is a very popular substitute for red in the summer.

- Water: Plenty, especially during the summer. Add a large pitcher or gallon of regular water if you don't want to serve straight from your kitchen tap.

- Seltzer: Sparkling water or club soda or whatever you call it. This is increasingly the most popular drink and mixer at my parties. People like hard seltzer too.

- Mixers: One liter of a juice mixer, such as cranberry or orange juice. One liter of cola.

- Ice: As needed. Buying a bag of ice is easier than

---

1   Temper your hate on screw-top bottles, wine snobs. I'm trying to keep this as easy as possible for new hosts.

making a bunch in the freezer. You could get a cooler to store your ice if you don't have freezer space.

For bonus points, buy two lemons or limes to slice up and leave by the bar area.

 PARTY PRO TIP
If you're drinking alcohol at your party, be mindful. Don't drink so much that you lose track of time and your personal goals in hosting.

A NOTE ABOUT BEER

You might be surprised that I haven't mentioned beer. There's a reason for this omission. I find beer difficult to serve. You need to chill it in advance, and it usually comes in single servings. Some beer drinkers are often highly brand-loyal as well.

It's easier for me to just not serve it. I haven't gotten any complaints. If you really want to serve beer, don't let me stop you. But know that I've hosted plenty of parties without beer simply because it makes my preparation easier.

Disposable Cups

Single-use plastics are bad for the environment, and while paper cups are a little better, they're still a waste. One day I hope to find a better solution. However, for a new host, disposable cups will make cleanup far easier. You'll be more likely to want to host again when you don't have a sink full of dirty cups and glasses to wash. This book is about making party hosting easy—if you feel strongly against using disposable cups, feel free to find your own solution. Otherwise, I recommend you use plastic cups for your first few parties.

 PARTY PRO TIP

Stay away from the red plastic cups beloved by American college frat parties. Those cups are unprofessional and ugly.

As a regular host who lived in an apartment without a dishwasher for thirteen years, I have strong opinions on disposable plastic cups. Here are my suggestions:

- Use clear cups that hold around ten ounces (300 mL).

- Purchase them in packs of fifty or a hundred. You'll have extras for your next party.

- Avoid cheap, flimsy plastic cups. To reduce waste, you want your guests to use the same cup all night.

- Leave two Sharpie markers near the bar and ask your guests to write their names on their cups. If someone is helping with the bar, tell them to write people's names on the cups *before* they pour a drink since it's nearly impossible to write with marker on a slightly wet plastic cup.

(www) For a list and photos of my favorite plastic cups, plus my ongoing tests to find a great paper or reusable option, visit www.party.pro/cups.

Serve Simple Snacks Only

Stick to the basics when choosing food. Buy these snacks a week before your party:

- **Chips:** salted tortilla or potato chips, two twelve- to fifteen-ounce bags (370 g). Add guacamole for bonus points.

- **Nuts:** salted peanuts, cashews, or mixed nuts, sixteen ounces (450 g).

- **Fruits and veggies:** grapes, two pounds (900 g). Baby carrots, one pound (450 g). Add hummus to dip.

- **Cheese plate:** two pounds (900 g), presliced or cubed. I rarely serve cheese, but several hosts I talked to suggested it. You could also add sliced meat, like

salami. Charcuterie boards photograph well. Just
keep it simple.

These snacks will make a big difference to hungry guests try-
ing to hold out until dinner. They are all easy to serve and
require almost no preparation.

> Perhaps you want to serve warm food at your party. Be
> careful. Before you know it, toasted walnuts have mor-
> phed into a determination to bring out baked brioche with
> homemade appetizers and a wine-tasting menu to match.
> I've seen this happen.
>
> You can certainly host a successful party that involves
> a lot of food. But you can also host an equally successful
> party with simple snacks. Add more options later when
> you become more comfortable. Perhaps you'll discover a
> signature snack that you love to serve for your guests to
> enjoy. But don't let food become a roadblock in hosting an
> easy, low-maintenance first party.

How to Prepare on the Day of the Party

Preparing your home for a party is easy. There are a few key
steps. Don't wait until the last minute to do these. Some can
even be done the day before.

Download a printable checklist of this section at
www.party.pro/print.

Declutter Any Rooms Guests Will Be In

Find one or more large plastic containers. Cardboard boxes
work too. The ones I use hold 30 quarts (28 liters) and mea-
sure 18 × 12 × 11.5 inches (46 × 31 × 29 cm). Walk around your
space and throw everything that doesn't need to be on display
into those containers. Then stash the containers out of sight.
Examples: electronics, toys, clothes, mail, magazines.

To quickly tidy my space, I put medicine, clothes, mail, and other random
items inside a plastic bin. Then I hide it in my closet until after the party.

Empty Your Trash Cans Before Your Party
Starts—and During if Needed

I've been to parties where the trash cans are completely full
an hour into the party. This is bad. Guests don't know what

to do with their trash. They'll leave it out in the open on a table nearby. Or they will hold onto it, using an empty cup or a dirty paper plate as a social crutch. Full garbage cans show that you're not a mindful host. Watch those cans during the party, or delegate the duty to a trusted friend.

Prep your Bathroom

Leave a lightly scented candle in your bathroom. Make sure there's a small trash can.

Clean Out Your Medicine Cabinet

Guests might be nosy. If there's anything in your medicine cabinet you don't want them to see, now's the time to put it away.

Remove Large Bath Towels from Your Bathroom

Leave only small hand towels. You don't want to use your bath towel after it has been touched by lots of people. Removing your body towels from your bathroom is a party pro move. If you don't have hand towels, leave some dishtowels or napkins in the bathroom.

Clean Surfaces

Wipe down your kitchen countertops and any tables you'll be using. Do a quick dusting if needed. You don't have to deep clean your apartment. But you also don't want it to be anywhere close to filthy.

Clean Out Your Refrigerator, Then Chill Your Mixers

Throw away old food or expired condiments. You will need the space if a guest brings any chilled beverages. Put mixers, sparkling water, and white wine in the refrigerator to cool down.

Create Your Bar Area

Set out your alcohol, mixers, ice, and cups right before your party starts. Make it an easy location for guests to access that's not near the entrance. Place a marker nearby to write names on cups. Place an empty cup on top of the ice to be used as a scoop.

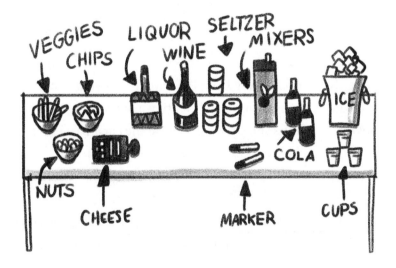

Snack and bar area. At my parties, I split this between two smaller tables. It helps break up the flow so everyone isn't crowding in one area.

Set Out the Snacks

My friend Liz shared this tip about snack preparation:

> "I often put out all the bowls and little serving dishes the
> night before with sticky notes to make sure I have some-
> thing for each item. It reminds me not to leave anything
> in the refrigerator. If I don't do this, I have forgotten one
> item and then get angry when I have to finish two bags of
> carrots on my own! This is also very helpful for last-min-
> ute preparation so that you're not scrambling to find an
> acceptable dish minutes before your guests arrive."

Right before the party starts, pour the chips, nuts, and veggies
into bowls. Do not serve them directly from the containers
they're packaged in.

Place these snacks away from the entrance of your space to
avoid guests congregating and creating a bottleneck. I like to
put a bowl of nuts and cheese plate near the bar area. I put the
chips, salsa, grapes, and carrots on a coffee table nearby.

Prep Your Music

Line up your playlist or streaming station and do a quick sound-
check. Start playing your music. Avoid these music mistakes:

 Don't: use a free streaming service that plays
commercials.

Don't: turn the music volume so loud it's hard for people to hear each other talk.

 Don't: waste time trying to curate a unique party playlist.

ABOUT THE SOUNDTRACK

Before my first guests arrive, I like to put on music. This also helps me to get into an upbeat party mood. Music is essential to hosting in your home. It fills the silence and builds atmosphere, especially when there are only a few guests at your party.

I usually stream the Beach Boys channel from a paid online music service like Spotify or Pandora. I love this channel because the music is timeless and appeals to a wide audience. Some other options are linked at www.party.pro/playlists. Whether you choose the Beach Boys or another theme, play music that's positive and uplifting yet still makes for good background sound. You want to fill the room with energy.

A Final Walkthrough Before Your Guests Arrive

Shortly before your party starts, walk through the entire experience you'll be providing. Stand outside and come in as though you were a guest arriving. Consider every step. What will your guests see as they arrive? What will they notice?

When you physically walk through the space, you might notice details you otherwise would have missed. Perhaps you forgot to throw some clutter into boxes or you haven't yet lit your bathroom candle. You may also find ways to make the space more welcoming.

 PARTY PRO TIP

Make a few handwritten messages to provide directions and motivation to your guests as they approach your party. Tape them somewhere visible: on your mailbox, door, or stairs leading to your home.

I love these simple signs and so do my guests. I post them up before every party. It's an easy way to add a bit of fun and personality and make people feel welcome.

Samantha's Story:
The Seeds of Procrastination

Samantha is a florist in New York City. When I spoke to her after her first party, she told me she'd waited until the day of the party to buy all of her supplies. Imagine: over a dozen guests are arriving to your home in a few hours and you don't have any cups, mixers, or even name tags. Totally unprepared. I would be so anxious. This is my personal version of hell.

Waiting until the last minute caused Samantha a massive amount of stress. A trip to the office supply store to buy name tags and searching for cups wasted valuable time and energy. By the time her guests arrived, she was tired, sweaty, and frazzled—hardly how she wanted to greet people. But at least she did have some great floral arrangements.

Samantha admitted that she tends to be a procrastinator, often waiting until the last minute to do things. She also told me that she'd learned her lesson. For her next party, she bought supplies well in advance. She ordered name tags, markers, and cups online. She bought her alcohol, mixers, and some nonperishable snacks a full week ahead. Doing that allowed her to minimize her preparation time and be more focused on making meaningful introductions during the party.

☑ CHAPTER CHECKLIST

☐ A week before your party, buy the necessary supplies.

☐ Download and print the basic party supplies shopping list, plus the "How to Prepare on the Day of the Party" checklist, at www.party.pro/print.

☐ One day before your party, review the section "How to Prepare on the Day of the Party." Start on any tasks that can be done early.

☐ On the day of your party, complete each of the items in the section "How to Prepare on the Day of the Party."

☐ Play music to set the mood.

☐ Walk inside and look at your space from the perspective of a guest. See if you can find any easy ways to make it more welcoming, like putting up a little welcome note.

PART 3

Party Time

EXAMPLE PARTY SCHEDULE

7:00 p.m. First guests begin to arrive. This is the Awkward Zone—Chapter 11.

7:10 p.m. Icebreaker 1 (Beginner)—Chapter 12.

7:15 p.m. *Unstructured time. You're doing great!*

7:40 p.m. Icebreaker 2 (Beginner, again)—Chapter 12.

7:50 p.m. *Unstructured time. Help guests mingle.*

8:20 p.m. Group photo, then Icebreaker 3 (Advanced)—Chapter 13.

8:30 p.m. *Unstructured time.*

9:00 p.m. Party ends—Chapter 14.

Navigating the First Twenty Minutes

The first twenty minutes of an event are the most stressful. I call this window of time the Awkward Zone. It's a phase almost every party passes through.

But you can prepare to navigate this period successfully. I'll help you avoid repeating the mistakes I had to learn the hard way. You'll see how to pass through the Awkward Zone with confidence and poise.

The Awkward Zone

Your party starts at 7:00 p.m. Three of your guests arrive at 7:00, but nobody else shows up until 7:15. Oh, and the three people who arrive exactly on time happen to be the three people whom you're least comfortable spending time with. They could be new coworkers, anxious friends, or someone's plus-one that you don't know well.

It happens. At this early stage, there aren't enough people at your event to build momentum and start the party energy organically. It could feel like everyone is waiting for something or that conversations are forced.

Now consider the Awkward Zone from the perspective of one of your guests. They arrive at your party and you're the only other person there. They will ask themselves where the rest of the guests are or if they had the wrong night. Is anyone else coming?

Don't blame yourself here. The Awkward Zone is awkward for everyone, not just first-time hosts. Even experienced hosts like me can be caught unaware.

 PARTY PRO TIP

Ask two trusted friends to arrive fifteen minutes early. They can help you set up and welcome guests.

Over time, I've come to love the challenge of the Awkward Zone. I know handling it well can set the tone for the whole party.

How I Used to Handle the
Awkward Zone (Hint: Poorly)

At one of the first parties I hosted, I was unprepared for the Awkward Zone. The first couple of guests to arrive were milling about while I scurried around my apartment taking care of last-minute preparations. At least I was wearing pants this time.

Soon a new acquaintance arrived. Because I was busy setting up, I quickly introduced her to the other attendees with the only detail I could remember. "Hey everybody," I said. "This is Jessica. She's Mormon."

It is an unspoken rule of polite American society that you don't talk about religion or politics with strangers or new friends. Nobody knew what to say because of my poor introduction. No one replied. It was dead quiet.

I ruined the moment and alienated a new friend. That's the danger of the Awkward Zone. Instead, I should have done a quick icebreaker to create a bond and introduce my first party guests.

On another occasion in my early days of hosting, I got lazy. I scheduled a party the day before. I reached out to several friends and told them I was having guests over the following night. "Come over any time from 6:00 p.m. until 10:00 p.m.," I said.

You already know I was asking for trouble. I should have used a longer runway, invited my core group first, and limited the party to only two hours to encourage more people to show up on time.

For the first hour of that party, there were only three people: me, my girlfriend, and one other guy that I only barely knew. I liked this guy, but I felt a real pressure to entertain him. This was a tough Awkward Zone and I handled it poorly. We stood in a triangle grasping at conversational threads. There was a lot of awkward silence. Convinced that someone could arrive any minute, I didn't allow myself to be present or settle into a genuine conversation.

 PARTY PRO TIP

The more people that show up to your party, the easier hosting becomes. More guests (within reason) equal less work for you to carry conversations.

Handle the Awkward Zone Like a Pro

A little awkwardness during the first several minutes is normal. We've all been to events with few attendees. Just play it cool. Your first arrivals will forgive you, and they won't sneak away to start a rival party.

Plus, now that you know about the Awkward Zone, you're already ahead of the game. These tips will show you how to handle it well. Don't stress. You're going to do great.

How to Welcome an Early Guest

The first thing to do is give special acknowledgment to guests who arrive at your party early or on time. Tell them how happy you are that they have arrived and celebrate that they're among the first few guests.

> Laura! Welcome! Oh wow, you are the first person to arrive. I am so glad you are here and that you're here first. Tonight is going to be a lot of fun.

Imagine your guests have never met you in person before. Maybe you reached out to them as you started hosting more parties to grow your network (great job!). Or they are coming as a guest of someone you've invited. Now think how special it will be for them to meet you for the first time with your face smiling and your eyes lit up.

When people arrive at my party, I do everything I can to present them with the most welcoming first impression. What I don't do is apologize for the lack of other guests. Avoid that mindset. It's a trap. Instead, celebrate the arrival of your first guests. Turn any hesitation into a moment of appreciation.

 Do: welcome your guests exuberantly and celebrate their arrival.

 Don't: apologize for a lack of other attendees.

Delegate Duties

Next, delegate some functions of the party to your early arrivals. Enlist them to help you make the party a success. For example, I often get someone to help me serve drinks. But I'm not asking them to tend bar all night. I'm giving them a way to contribute and connect with new arrivals.

I've found that some guests like having something to do. Early arrivals especially appreciate the chance to feel useful instead of making idle conversation. The number one thing I hear from guests who turn up early is "How can I help?" When I tell them exactly how they *can* help, most are pleasantly surprised by my directness and are delighted to pitch in.

First, explain what you need:

> Laura, since you're here now, can you please help me with something? It would be a big help if you stand by the bar area and get drinks for the first few guests who arrive.

Then, when more people arrive, you'll welcome them, give them a name tag, and send them over to Laura so she can help get them a drink. Instead of feeling like an unfortunate early arrival, now Laura feels empowered.

LAURA AS FIRST GUEST

LAURA AS A SUPERHERO

Brian Quinn, Editorial Director of Events at Skift and an experienced party host, told me about the benefits guests receive when they help with drinks:

> "By being a volunteer bartender for the first few minutes, the person gets to meet and greet everyone that arrives with something they'll be excited about. Serving someone a drink is an instant and easy way to strike up a conversation. The person in this role should convey enthusiasm and hospitality. They become an extension of you as a host. However, not everyone is comfortable with that task. If the person you delegate looks like they are not enjoying the job, ask if they'd rather swap out with someone else."

Brian's right. This "delegate duties" approach may not work for everyone. Some people won't know how to serve even a glass of wine. In that case, you can assign them a different task. Certain guests may not wish to carry out *any* task. If it happens, don't try to force them. Say, "No worries. Let's just hang out. Make yourself at home." Then ask someone else to help you.

Almost any party duty can be delegated. In addition to helping with drinks, each of these tasks gives guests an opportunity to interact:

- coat and bag check

- writing guests' first names on their beverage cups with marker

- snack support: setup and refills

- party photographer

- conversation starter: help others say hi to someone new

Pick someone outgoing and confident to be a connector. Ask them to say hi to all of the guests and include others in their conversations.

Tyler's Story: Spicing It Up

Remember Tyler in Little Rock, that guy who started with no network and now has a long waiting list for his parties? He uses delegation well. He enlists his early arrivals in creative ways. For example, he appoints one person to be in charge of high fives. His opening line might be, "Go see Darren at the bar to get a drink, and then see Gina for your free high five."

When the party gets going and more people arrive, he asks someone to be the official photographer. It's a simple, fun way to get guests involved in the party. He loves seeing the photos later because he rarely takes any himself.

Don't worry about imposing on your guests. When you ask them to help, guests will feel invested in your party. They will take responsibility for its success and help you navigate and exit the Awkward Zone.

Ending the Awkward Zone

The Awkward Zone normally ends after four or five guests arrive and you start your first icebreaker for early arrivals.

The easiest way to end it quicker is to have more of your guests show up on time. Thankfully, when you host a 2-hour cocktail party, the compressed timeline will naturally minimize your Awkward Zone.

 PARTY PRO TIP

If you're still feeling anxious about how your party will start, ask two people in your core group to arrive fifteen minutes early to help you start strong.

Your first icebreaker is coming up next. Icebreakers are the most interesting bit of your party. You should feel some excitement as you exit the Awkward Zone.

Introducing the Party Harmonica

You probably saw a harmonica in the list of supplies to buy for your party. Perhaps you thought: *What's the deal with the harmonica? Isn't that weird?*

It could look that way, I'll admit. But there's a reason I use this. The harmonica serves to gracefully get the attention of the group to start your icebreakers.

You might not think that you need a party harmonica. You probably think it sounds corny or even downright childish. Perhaps you think you have a loud voice and you won't need it. But when you have fifteen people in your home and everyone is talking at the same time, you'll appreciate how easy and smooth a harmonica makes it to get people's attention.

There are alternatives. You could have a dinner bell or small xylophone set (even more ridiculous). Some people knock a fork against a glass or use a whistle.

Other options for calling attention at your party.

I prefer a harmonica. The tone is pleasing, and it attracts attention without being loud or abrasive. It's less formal than a dinner bell and more portable than a xylophone. When your guests hear your harmonica, they know something fun is about to go down. They'll look to you for what happens next.

I don't play a song or even a few notes when I use my harmonica. I just blow out, usually on the low side of the scale, in one exhale for three to four seconds. (Yes, I timed it.)

[www] Video example: See how to use your party harmonica at www.party.pro/video1.

You can also scale the volume of a harmonica much easier than clanking a glass. Start with a gentle, low tone to get people's attention. Blow a bit harder and higher to call for quiet.

Get a Party Harmonica—But Don't Just Take My Word for It

Maybe you're still not convinced. Listen to these people who all read early drafts of this book and then hosted their first parties:

> "I was hesitant to use the harmonica because it seemed silly. But with all the noise during our parties, the harmonica got everyone's attention quickly. It lightened the mood for icebreakers."
>
> —Chris Fowles, Partner & Technical Director, Washington, D.C.

> "I didn't buy a harmonica for my first party, and I regretted it later. I had to yell to get people's attention. That yelling killed the great vibe we were trying to create with the party in the first place. Don't skip on this. A harmonica is the chef's kiss to hosting a fantastic party."
>
> —Mary Beth Yale, Literary Consultant, Mexico City

> "Once, I used a whistle for a large party, and it was too much. It worked, but it was jarring. After that, I've always

used a harmonica. Guests find it funny, but it's very effective. A cheap harmonica can get a group to pause their conversations and listen to what's next."

—Tyler Vawser, Vice President of People, Little Rock

"At first, I was hesitant to buy a harmonica because I thought it would make me look weird. But after I followed Nick's advice and got one, instead of raising my voice to quiet the room for icebreakers, I used the harmonica. It worked so much better and sounded a lot more peaceful than if I were to yell over everyone talking! I look much more in control with the harmonica. It's become an expected and accepted part of my parties."

—Nagina Sethi Abdullah, CEO and Founder, Jersey City

☑ CHAPTER CHECKLIST

☐ Write down on an index card what jobs you can delegate to early guests. Tape this card near the front door so you'll see it when the first people arrive.

☐ Warmly welcome each of your guests and celebrate their arrival. Give everyone a name tag.

☐ Delegate a few tasks like bartending and coat check.

☐ When four or five people have arrived, prepare to exit the Awkward Zone by starting your first icebreaker.

☐ Get a harmonica. You'll be using it to help summon everyone together for your icebreakers in the next chapter.

CHAPTER 12

Beginner Icebreakers

I like to use my parties to bring together a diverse group of people. One party in particular included work colleagues, people I knew from the gym, and a range of artists and performers.

Naturally there was some tension in the room at the start of the night. But no one exemplified that tension more than Diane. Right away, Diane stood out as a grizzled New Yorker. Wearing all black with a slight scowl, she looked as though she had run away from middle school and lived on the mean streets of Manhattan until she was discovered as a savage fashion critic.

We circled up and I introduced my favorite beginner ice-breaker: "What's one of your favorite things that you eat for breakfast?" I went first and asked Diane if she would go next. When it was her turn, she said:

"My name's Diane. I live here in New York. I'm a writer. My favorite thing for breakfast is cigarettes."

The introduction fit her perfectly. Her dry sense of humor made everyone laugh, breaking the tension in the room. By being self-deprecating and expressing a little vulnerability, she became more human and easier for others to approach.

Other guests followed Diane's lead and poked fun at themselves. Her humor and vulnerability were contagious. The room loosened up and started to come together in fun harmony. It felt like we were all experiencing something special as each person introduced themselves.

That's the feeling a good icebreaker creates. When you host these types of parties, your guests will feel that they're a part of something special.

Why Icebreakers Work So Well

I'm sure you've been to parties where you sense that there are a lot of interesting people in the room. But you don't know who they are or how to connect with them. You wander around hoping to get lucky enough to meet someone interesting. Or maybe you've felt how hard it can be to approach strangers or join an active conversation.

When the host facilitates icebreakers, it changes everything! Icebreakers massively improve the odds of new connections and conversations.

Good icebreakers are like a short survey of the party where everyone gets to see the results in real time. Each guest broadcasts who they are and finds out more about the other people present. You get to quickly "meet" and learn about everyone in the room.

Icebreakers are like a short survey of the party. They help your guests meet more people.

Icebreakers at your party will serve as both an introduction and a conversation starter. Following my formula, you'll use them three different times at your party to help your guests create new connections. They'll take five to ten minutes to complete, and each time, they'll give your guests an excuse to approach one another.

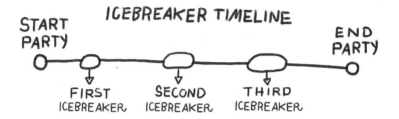

For a party that starts at 7:00 p.m., do icebreakers
at approximately 7:10, 7:40, and 8:20 p.m.

But let me be clear: icebreakers aren't a substitute for real conversation. They're just a shortcut to help your guests feel more comfortable making that first contact.

I know this part sounds tough. Some people are afraid of stopping their party to lead icebreakers. That's totally normal. You're going to do fine even if you forget a few of the steps I'm about to discuss. Once you try out icebreakers at your party, you'll get the hang of it. Then you'll never want to host another gathering without them.

Choosing the Right Icebreaker

Not all icebreakers are created equal. People often tell me they love icebreakers only to say that their favorite one is something dramatic like: "What's your biggest fear?" or "What was the worst date you ever went on?"

Those are terrible icebreakers. They require a deep level of vulnerability and openness. Most people aren't ready for that at the start of a casual 2-hour cocktail party.

THE ICEBREAKER STRUCTURE

Everyone will answer these three questions for each round of icebreakers:

1. What's your name?
2. What do you do for work?[1]
3. (The icebreaker question)

Stick to simple, fun icebreakers that are quick to answer. Ask your guests to gather in a circle. Have everyone say their name, their profession, and what one of their favorite things is to eat for breakfast.

Some people tell me that icebreakers like this are childish. They say they haven't done icebreakers since fourth grade, so why should they start now? However, after hosting hundreds of parties, simple icebreakers have helped me warm up the room—*every single time*. Starting your party with an icebreaker

---

1   It is perfectly reasonable to hate the idea of asking someone about their work at a party among friends. Read about why I think it is important, plus a few alternative ways to ask this question with grace, in Chapter 13.

like the favorite breakfast question works because it gives people a chance to speak in a no-stress, structured format.

Breakfast Is the Icebreaker of Champions

You might still be wondering about the relevance of asking people to name their favorite breakfast food. A simple question like this at the start of your party makes people relatable. By asking people to talk about their favorite breakfast food, you're getting them to share something personal that they enjoy in a casual context. Everyone knows what they like to eat for breakfast.[1] It is the most ritualistic of meals. What we eat for breakfast doesn't define us as people even though it reveals a little bit about our personality.

For example, if one guest says, "Cereal with blueberries and almond milk," there's a good chance they're into healthy eating. Or if someone swears by pancakes and bacon slathered in maple syrup, they might be the person to ask for delicious restaurant recommendations.

---

1   Intermittent fasting, or "skipping breakfast" as my grandparents called it, has become more popular over the past few years. Don't let this dissuade you from asking the favorite breakfast food icebreaker.

I've tested this icebreaker extensively. It might sound boring, but it is safe. It works nearly 100 percent of the time for almost 100 percent of guests. It's practically impossible for it to go wrong and it sets you and your party up for success.

You'll use this same icebreaker twice: first to practice with your four or five early arrivals, then approximately twenty-five minutes later with the whole party.

Other Beginner Icebreaker Options

If you're determined to vary the "What's your favorite thing to eat for breakfast?" question, here are three other options:

- What was the first job that you ever got paid to do?

- What was your first online screen name and why did you choose it?

- What's one of your favorite drinks, with or without alcohol?

I'm only listing three because these are all you need to get started with hosting parties. I've used the same beginner icebreaker hundreds of times. I don't try to use a new one at every party, even if my guests have heard that same icebreaker at my last party.

Party People in Action: Sean Oliver

Product Marketing Manager at Microsoft in Seattle, Washington

---

Nick: How do you do icebreakers at your parties?

Sean: At my first party, four folks showed up in the first fifteen minutes. I made them the 'Early Arrivals Squad' and we did the favorite breakfast icebreaker. I put icebreaker windows on my calendar about twenty-five to thirty minutes apart. I did the breakfast icebreaker again, then finished the night with "What's the best thing you've purchased in the past year?"

Nick: What have you gained by hosting parties?

Sean: Everyone asked to be invited to the next one. Throwing it was far easier than my earlier efforts. I got to see my friends become friends! I even co-hosted a work event the very next day and used these techniques to smooth out some of the kinks.

Nick: What advice do you have to new hosts?

Sean: Folks *love* guacamole and chips.

How to Facilitate the First Icebreaker

It's the night of your first party. You're almost out of the Awkward Zone as four or five people have arrived. Grab your party harmonica because this is the first time that you get to use it. Turn down the music, blow a long note into your harmonica to get the group's attention, and say something upbeat like this:

> OK everybody. What a great group of friends! Let's come over here to circle up and stand together. You all showed up early or right on time. Thank you for that. You're great.

Have everyone come together and stand in a circle. Then introduce the first icebreaker:

> I want us to go around the circle and do a quick icebreaker so we can get a survey of who's here. Say your name, what you do for work, and what one of your favorite things to eat for breakfast is. If you don't want to talk about work, you can say something you're passionate about instead— like a hobby or charity.

You'll go first in answering the icebreaker. But first, look to the person to your left or right and ask for their permission to go next in the sequence by saying, "I'll go first, and then can I go to you?" If they agree, say again:

> Great. So, I'll go first, and then I'll go to you, and we'll go around the circle in that same direction.

Clearly outlining how the icebreaker will flow and in which direction will reduce anxiety among introverts and help everyone to be prepared for when it is their turn.

 Do: go first in answering the icebreaker.

 Do: ask permission for who to go next.

 Don't: call on someone unexpectedly.

Sample Icebreaker Answer

Now you will go first and set the example for how people should speak their part. My short but juicy answer to the breakfast icebreaker is:

> My name is Nick Gray. I'm the Founder of Museum Hack, a company that does renegade museum tours in New York City and at some of the best museums in America. My favorite thing to eat for breakfast is scrambled eggs with spinach, but I have a secret ingredient—I use coconut oil.

By including a bit about my company and a "secret ingredient" in my breakfast answer, I invite others to share more vivid or detailed descriptions. That icebreaker answer takes me twenty-five seconds to say. It is short but not too short. Answers to icebreakers at your party should be thirty seconds or less. You don't want your guests to start telling their full life stories just yet.

A good icebreaker is a fast icebreaker. Thirty seconds is a good limit for someone's answer.

Start the icebreaker now. You're going to do great!

 Do: move quickly from person to person.

 Don't: let people ask follow-up questions during the icebreaker time.

 PARTY PRO TIP

If a guest arrives in the middle of an icebreaker, bring them into the circle and have the new person go last. Get them a name tag afterward.

RECAP: STEPS TO START THE FIRST ICEBREAKER

1. Turn down the music and sound a note with your party harmonica.
2. Gather your guests into a circle.
3. Announce the first icebreaker. Say that you'll go first. Ask the person to your right or left: "Then can I go to you?"
4. Remind the group again of the three elements of the icebreaker (name, what you do for work, and the icebreaker question), say you'll go first, then indicate which direction around the circle.
5. Start the icebreaker: "OK then! Here we go. My name is Nick, for work I..."

What to Do After the Last Person Closes the Icebreaker

Say this to facilitate the transition out of icebreakers:

> Thank you. Great job everyone. We just did this icebreaker, and there are great people here and more coming soon. Go make yourself a drink, say hi to someone new, and we'll do another icebreaker in about twenty minutes.

And then—bingo—that's it. That's how your party transitions into and out of your first icebreaker.

Hey, you just did your first round of icebreakers. Nice work! That's the most complicated thing you'll ever have to do at a party. But it pays major dividends. And don't worry if you forget a step or two.

Now the party goes back to people mingling and talking, like what happens at most gatherings. Allow your guests to self-organize for a while in this unstructured time. Think of this moment as confirmation that you've survived the Awkward Zone. Congratulations!

How Many Icebreakers and How Often?

Do two beginner icebreakers (same questions) and then one advanced icebreaker at your party. No more, no less. Stop for icebreakers approximately every thirty minutes. Set a timer to remind yourself.

Carry out the first icebreaker with the first four or five people who show up. Twenty minutes later, when most of your guests have arrived, you'll introduce the same icebreaker again. Early guests won't complain about repeating their information in the same icebreaker. They will understand that you are doing it again because there are now more people at your party. Thirty minutes later, you'll do one advanced icebreaker that allows your guests to share deeper and strike up even more new conversations.

DETAILED EXAMPLE PARTY SCHEDULE

7:00 p.m. First guests begin to arrive. Awkward Zone. Warmly welcome. Delegate duties.

7:10 p.m. Icebreaker 1, beginner icebreaker for early arrivals: name, what you do for work, favorite breakfast.

7:15 p.m. *Unstructured time begins. Awkward Zone ends. You're doing great!*

7:40 p.m. Icebreaker 2, beginner icebreaker again, but now with more people: name, what you do for work, favorite breakfast.

7:50 p.m. *Unstructured time. Help guests mingle and make introductions.*

8:20 p.m. Group photo. Then: icebreaker 3, advanced icebreaker.

8:30 p.m. *Unstructured time. Help guests mingle and make introductions.*

8:50 p.m. Announce party ending soon.

9:00 p.m. Party ends. Tell everyone you need your beauty rest and they can continue celebrating at a nearby bar or restaurant.

How Icebreakers Shuffle the Room
and Help Guests Circulate

Icebreakers have a hidden feature: they break up conversations.

Have you ever attended a party and found yourself stuck talking to a person that you're not particularly enjoying? Perhaps you felt it would be rude to end the conversation and walk away.

Well, icebreakers will do that. They give everyone a great reason to move on from a conversation and then chat with someone new.

When you stop your party to do icebreakers, you'll have to interrupt a few conversations. I remember how nervous I was to do this the first time. I thought: *Things are going so well! Everyone is talking. Why would I want to stop their conversations?*

Recently, I tested this theory. It was time do to do the first round of icebreakers at my party. After gently sounding my party harmonica, I found myself walking up to a high-profile guest who was still engaged in a discussion. I didn't know him too well, and by interrupting his conversation and inviting him to the icebreaker, I was putting myself at risk of being rejected.

Did I hesitate? Maybe for a few seconds. But I did it. He joined the icebreaker with all the other guests, and it was great. It reminded me that my job as a host is to shuffle the room and encourage new conversations. If guests want to continue their conversation later, they will. **Your loyalty as a host is not to a single guest but to the party as a whole.** So be confident when you start your icebreaker and ask everyone to join.

 **Video example:** To see what it looks like for a host to pause the party and start an icebreaker, visit www.party.pro/video1.

Do: be playful in your interruptions. Use your harmonica.

Don't: wait idly for the end of every conversation.

Don't: be afraid to interrupt to start a round of icebreakers.

☑ CHAPTER CHECKLIST

☐ Practice explaining the icebreakers out loud, including asking a person if they will go after you.

☐ Practice your own answer to the icebreakers so that you are ready to go first during your party and can lead with a strong example. Don't worry if you make a mistake or stumble over a word. This signals to your guests that this is perfectly fine.

☐ Plan at what times during your party you'll call everyone together to do icebreakers.

☐ When four to five guests have arrived, start your first icebreaker. It is a great chance to practice, and you'll create a connection with your early arrivals. Turn down the music, sound your harmonica, and form a circle to begin.

☐ Forty minutes after your party was scheduled to begin, do the same beginner icebreaker—but now including everyone at the party. This is your second icebreaker.

☐   If you're nervous, have a friend stand next to you.
Ask them to follow your lead after you start the
icebreaker.

High five! You're doing great.

CHAPTER 13

Advanced Icebreakers and Bonus Techniques

I hope you're becoming excited about the concept of icebreakers. Perhaps you're already dreaming up your own. Nice! Keep in mind that a good beginner icebreaker is an easy question with an immediate, definitive answer. Don't ask your guests brain teasers or interesting questions yet. Those types of icebreakers at the start of a gathering require your guests to do too much work to come up with an answer.

For example: "What's your favorite book?"

Is that a good icebreaker?

It might seem that way, but it actually takes a lot of thought. I can't name my absolute favorite book right away. I could name a few books that I like, but picking my exact favorite is a difficult decision. I'd obsess about picking the best possible book to make me sound smart or interesting.[1]

The breakfast icebreaker is good and safe because you eat (or decide not to eat) breakfast every day. It doesn't take long to decide on your favorite breakfast food. You may have even thought about it this morning.

Beginner icebreakers are easy for your guests
to answer. No brain teasers, please.

After hosting a few parties using my formula, Jay Irwin from Brooklyn chose to modify his beginner icebreaker question by

---

1   The way to modify "What's your favorite book?" to be a good icebreaker would be to say, "What's a book that you've read recently?" That takes away the pressure of picking an absolute favorite and makes it easier to have a quick answer.

asking people to name their favorite vice. He decided his friends could handle a prompt edgier than breakfast foods. "It worked really well," he told me. "It got my friends to share something deeper about themselves, and guests with similar answers had an easy conversation starter for the time between icebreakers."

Only Use Positive Icebreakers

One of my colleagues, Dustin Growick, provides a brilliant demonstration of how icebreakers can go wrong.

When a group of us at a museum conference in Arizona went out to a Mexican restaurant, I suggested that we do an icebreaker. Dustin volunteered to lead it. This is what he said:

> "Let's go around the circle, say your name, say which museum you work at and what you do there, and then point to a scar on your body and tell us how you got it."

Dustin did a great job sticking to the overall icebreaker structure of name, work, and question. But can you see why this was a terrible question to ask? It got people into the wrong frame of mind. The attendees shared stories about unfortunate bike wrecks and car crashes, a few of which were very sad. As a participant, I felt uncomfortable listening to such intimate stories of misfortune from people I barely knew. The atmosphere quickly became heavy.

Dustin and I still joke about this story. But it wasn't so funny when it happened. Talking about a negative life experience at the start of our gathering was a downer for a group of museum nerds. It shifted the tone in the wrong direction. The same goes for asking about the worst first date someone has ever been on. This type of icebreaker may be hilarious with an intimate group of close friends, but at your 2-hour cocktail party of acquaintances, keep your icebreakers positive to help make more comfortable conversations.

Party People in Action: Jay Irwin

Director of Product Management at a
Technology Company in Brooklyn, New York

Nick: Why did you decide to start hosting parties?
Jay: I've hosted random parties before, but they never had any real structure to them. I used this book as an opportunity to get to know new people.

Nick: What happens at your parties?
Jay: I hold my parties in my apartment in Williamsburg, Brooklyn. It's got a big, open living room that's great for it. My parties are always on Tuesdays or Wednesdays. Those nights usually aren't too busy for people. I'm an irreverent guy, so I like to add some edginess to my icebreakers. Getting people a little out of their comfort zone is fun for me.

Nick: What's the biggest challenge or fear you've faced hosting parties?

Jay: I really haven't had a lot of big challenges. One annoying thing was a guest who drank too much alcohol and tried to be overly snarky during icebreakers. I cut their turn short during the second round, which was a bit awkward, but I think the other guests appreciated it.

Nick: What have you gained by hosting parties?

Jay: What I love about the system in this book is that it guarantees that party attendees won't be bored. The icebreakers give guests easy topics to chat about. I've also been able to co-host a party with a friend of mine who's in a band. He's got a totally different network than me, but since he's an awesome guy, I knew he'd invite interesting people. It was a lot of fun and I got to meet people with backgrounds in the arts who I otherwise wouldn't have met.

Advanced Icebreakers

You'll use one advanced icebreaker as your third and final icebreaker. Start it about forty minutes before the end of your party. The purpose of this icebreaker is to share interesting information among guests. Ideally, the information shared in the icebreaker can benefit others.

Advanced icebreakers maintain the same basic structure as beginner icebreakers, but they are more challenging. They're not scratch-your-head, furrow-your-brow challenging, but they demand a bit more thought from guests in crafting a reply.

If icebreakers set the stage for people to express themselves, then advanced icebreakers invite people to dig deeper.

My favorite advanced icebreaker and the one I recommend you use is:

> What's a great piece of media that you've consumed recently, and what did you like about it?

We've all listened to a podcast, read something interesting, or watched a good show. With so much media available, everyone at your party will have something different to share. Answers could include a movie, book, magazine article, Netflix show, YouTube video, TED Talk, or podcast.

Here's how to set this up for success at your party: Forty-five minutes before your party is scheduled to end, sound your harmonica, and give the group a warning that it is almost ice-breaker time. Tell them the question you're going to ask. This allows time to prepare an answer, get another drink, or use the restroom. I've used this announcement in the past:

Hey everyone! Good evening! It makes me so happy to see everyone having conversations. In about five minutes, we're going to do our last and final icebreaker of the night. I'm going to tell you the question in case you need a minute to prepare or think about it. The question will be: What's a great piece of media you consumed recently, and what did you like about it? It could be a podcast, a movie, an article, a great book, a fun reality TV show, whatever. Something that made you think or that you want to share. I'll sound my harmonica again in a few minutes to circle up, and we'll also do a group photo then. For now, grab another drink or freshen up. I'll be back in a few minutes.

Turn the music volume back up for a song or two as the group shuffles about. Five minutes later, start your last icebreaker. Bring the group together again in a circle. Take a quick group photo. Then remind them of the icebreaker question and in which way it will go around the circle.

We're going to go around the circle again for this last round of icebreakers. Say your name, tell us again what you do for work or something you're passionate about, and then tell us about a great piece of media that you've consumed recently and what you liked about it. It could be in the last month or however long. That could be a movie, book, magazine article, TV show, etc. Something fun or that made you think or that you want to share. I'll go first...

Guests repeat their name and occupation again, even if they did so at the last icebreaker. Repeating these things helps to remind others and create new connections for any late arrivals.

Guests standing in a circle for the icebreaker.

When you ask the advanced icebreaker, you ideally want your guests to share a little about who they are. If they have a guilty pleasure in watching a trashy reality television show, you hope that they'll feel comfortable sharing that. This is why advanced icebreakers work best later in your party schedule when guests have already built some rapport and loosened up.

Two More Advanced Icebreakers to Try

Here's another example: I sat down for a group dinner after an all-day business meeting with other CEOs. After we'd ordered, I proposed an icebreaker. My question was:

> What's one of the best things that you have purchased in the last year?

I explained that this could be anything from a kitchen appliance to a favorite book. It could even be an experience like a gym class or vacation.

Everyone shared their answers. One guy stood up and said his favorite recent purchase was a pair of men's stretchy jeans. They were mostly denim, with 5 percent spandex. Another guy sitting at the table who had tried a pair agreed with him. The guy who owned the jeans demonstrated how easily he could squat in them. Someone else joined in and showed off their jeans by parading around the outside of the dinner table. It turned into a fashion show at dinner. Everyone was having fun with it.

This moment would never have happened without an icebreaker. These CEOs used the framework of the icebreaker as a stage to share and express their personalities. It created a new level of connection among us.

Another great advanced icebreaker is:

> What's one of your favorite secret spots or life hacks for this city?

This can refer to restaurants, traffic shortcuts, amazing thrift stores, bars with great live music, or anything else special that guests want to share about their city.

Even More Advanced Icebreakers

- What's a compliment someone gave you that you still think about?

- If you were to do a citywide poll, what would you want to learn?

- What's one great habit that you're proud of, and how did you develop it?

- Do you have a favorite charity that you wish more people knew about?

- If you could teach a class about one topic that you're passionate about or an expert on, what would it be?

If you want a longer list of advanced icebreakers, I will send you more of my favorites. Email me at nick@party.pro.

Take a Group Photo

Most new hosts cherish a group photo. They see it and are incredibly proud of bringing everyone together. You can use your photo in a "Thanks for coming to my party" follow-up email the next day. You can also use a group photo as social proof when you reach out to invite guests to your next party.

 PARTY PRO TIP
A great time to take a group photo is immediately after you form the circle for your advanced icebreaker.

You'll be happy you took a group photo at your party. It's easy to forget, so make a reminder or ask someone to help.

To get everyone together for a picture, I hold my phone up and say "I want to take a quick group photo! Everyone look this way because I'm taking a selfie." I say this smiling and with high energy. I usually take a selfie so that it is quick and fun. If someone doesn't want to be in the picture, I ask them to take the group photo with my phone. Then we begin the last icebreaker.

Bonus Techniques

Try some of these tips if you're ready to improve your ice-breaker skills.

FIND YOUR HAPPY PLACE

If you're feeling nervous or overwhelmed as a first-time host, don't feel obligated to master all of the tips in this chapter. They are not required for a great gathering, and my formula is not "all or nothing." In fact, you already know enough to get going with your first party. You've already taken the most important steps to bring people together. Your first party is going to be great. You can always come back later and improve your skills, picking up where you left off.

Sharing the "Why" of Icebreakers

People are more engaged when they understand the purpose for an activity. Before you introduce an icebreaker, let your guests know the reason you're doing them.

Here's what I say:

> I'm so happy to have you all here. The reason I like to do
> these icebreakers is that I want you all to meet and talk
> to more people at my party. Maybe you'll hear something
> neat that inspires you to strike up a new conversation.
> Now, I'll go first...

Keep Up the Pace

Fast icebreakers will inject energy into your party. Don't allow
guests to talk for too long or ask follow-up questions during
the icebreaker. Each person should only talk for ten to thirty
seconds. If someone is running long, sound your harmonica
and tell them they have ten seconds to wrap it up.

Never Sit Down

An easy way to keep icebreakers short and raise the energy is to
have everyone stand in a tight circle. Some new hosts encourage
or allow their guests to sit down because they want people to be
comfortable. But this is a total buzzkill. Don't do it. Remember,
sitting down encourages guests to talk for too long and drops
the energy in the room when we're looking to boost it.

 PARTY PRO TIP

Always ask your guests to stand for icebreakers.
Remove chairs if needed and ask anyone who is
sitting and is able to stand and join the circle.

Cut Someone Off When They Talk Too Much

What happens if someone rambles on too long with their response to the icebreaker? Or if another person starts asking follow-up questions during the icebreaker? You'll simply signal to them, perhaps using your words and your harmonica, to wrap up and move on.[1]

Don't be afraid to cut people off if their icebreaker answer is too long.

New hosts are often scared of interrupting. Cutting people off can feel rude. But sometimes you need to be a little rude to one person to make the party better for the whole group.

Cut people off when necessary. It's your job as a host to protect the experience of everyone at the party.

---

1   Keep it positive. Don't use the finger-across-the-neck or throat-slitting motion.

When Kristin in North Carolina struggled to cut people off at her first party, one of her icebreakers took nearly a full hour. People sat down, asked follow-up questions, and gave long answers outside of the icebreaker formula. As a host, you need a sense of urgency. Icebreakers should create a rush of energy that guests take back into new conversations during unstructured time.

I suggested to Kristin that during her next icebreaker, she should position herself directly next to her husband. She secretly asked him to talk for too long during his ice-breaker answer just so she could practice gently blowing her harmonica, telling him to wrap it up, and then moving on to the next person. It worked perfectly: people laughed when she "scolded" him and then nobody rambled on.

PARTY PRO TIP

If you're worried about cutting someone off, you can toot your harmonica and say something like "Ten seconds left!" while they're speaking. Giving them time to wrap up sounds more like an expression of a universal rule and less like a personal attack.

`www` Video example: See me cut someone off during a party and exactly how I do it at www.party.pro/video2.

Always Ask about Employment—But Give an Option for the Unemployed or Embarrassed

It is helpful, for professional purposes, to know what somebody's job is and where they work. Include the questions "What's your name?" and "What do you do for work?" as the first parts of every icebreaker you lead.

But this question of "What do you do for work?" could be uncomfortable for the unemployed or people who are embarrassed by their jobs. So offer them an easy option to participate: let them name a hobby or charity they support instead.

Here's how I do that when I introduce my icebreakers:

> Tell us your name, what you do for work, and [icebreaker here]. If you don't want to talk about work, share something that you're really passionate about, like a hobby or charity you love.

I've found that small addition fixes any resistance. And it gives your guests the gift of being able to meet someone new for professional reasons.

Ask people to say what they do for work, even if you're just hosting a casual party with friends. You never know who is considering a career change or looking for a new job. Even if you already know what everybody does for work, I bet every-one else at your party doesn't. Remember that most people find out about new jobs, career opportunities, and clients from weak ties and loose connections.

Other Ways to Ask about Work

- How do you spend your days?

- What are you working on these days?

- What are you working on that you're most excited about right now?

- What's your professional mission?

- Where would we find you on Tuesday at 3:00 p.m.?

The Post-Icebreaker Void

After an icebreaker finishes, you may notice an empty feeling in the room. You're going from a structured activity to unstructured time. Suddenly there's no one in charge.

Don't worry. It takes a few seconds for guests to absorb the power and energy from the icebreaker back into themselves and then start new conversations. This is completely normal.

PARTY PRO TIP

Resist the temptation to facilitate another
icebreaker straight away.

Allow your guests to mingle organically. Regan Starr in Bloomington, Indiana says that he tells his guests to "Go make yourself another drink" right before he turns up the music. He says that to naturally add motion to the room, which helps fill the energy gap. I do the same thing at my parties. It gives people an excuse to get a fresh beverage, continue talking to the person next to them, or approach someone new who they want to meet after the icebreaker.

Then make yourself scarce for a few minutes. Go to the bathroom, the bar area, or the kitchen. Give the group time. Soon your guests will naturally break out of the icebreaker circle. You'll hear the volume of conversations rise as people begin talking to each other again.

SEVEN STEPS TO NEXT-LEVEL ICEBREAKERS

An ultra-experienced party host and icebreaker facilitator knows how to do the following:

1. Physically organize the crowd into a circle.
2. Make eye contact and project their voice confidently to the group.

3. State the "why" of doing icebreakers.

4. Model a good answer by going first.

5. Choose someone to go next, ask permission, and announce the plan.

6. Cut people off or speed them up if they take too long.

7. Make a concluding statement and handle the awkward atmosphere that develops directly after an icebreaker.

The Final Word on Icebreakers

Yes, using icebreakers may initially feel formulaic or scary. They may seem like a lot of work. But they're worth the effort. Icebreakers add good structure to your party. They help make new conversations easier and give your gathering more purpose. You'll be seen as someone who brings people together well. Even if you forget a few of the steps, your guests will respect and appreciate your efforts when you do icebreakers at your party. You are becoming such a great host now!

☑ CHAPTER CHECKLIST

☐   Forty-five minutes before your party is scheduled to end, give your guests an overview of the upcoming advanced icebreaker. Tell them the question that you will ask. Then encourage them to get another drink or freshen up.

☐   Five minutes later, bring your group together in a circle. Take a quick group photo. Then start the advanced icebreaker.

☐   Listen to all of the great answers as your guests go around the circle. Don't allow anyone to talk for too long. Keep the pace moving to maintain a high energy level.

☐   Review the list of bonus techniques when you're ready to improve your icebreaker facilitation skills.

☐   After the last person answers the icebreaker, thank everyone. Turn the music volume back up. Allow new conversations to naturally form in unstructured time. Enjoy the sounds of the connections you're helping to create.

CHAPTER 14

Ending on a High Note

Have you ever been one of the last to leave a dying party? You can feel the excitement drain out of the room.

Ending a party is like letting air out of a balloon. You can do it slowly, so the balloon gradually loses energy and becomes floppy. Or you can do it quickly, so the balloon makes a lot of noise, whizzes around, or even pops. Trust me—you want to do it quickly.

At the end of your party, guests will still be talking and making connections. It might even feel like the height of the night as you hear happy conversations and see people exchanging contact information.

End your party quickly and confidently. Accept the impermanence of it.

It won't feel natural to ask guests to leave or to end your party on time. To some, it might be the scariest part of hosting. But don't worry. After hosting and ending hundreds of parties, I've never lost a friendship or ruined a connection by ending on time. In fact, this tactic of ending a party is so effective that I've occasionally received Thank You notes from new guests. They tell me how refreshing it was to attend a party with structure that ended smoothly.

 PARTY PRO TIP
Resist the urge to let your first party run late. *This is a common new-host tendency and easy mistake to make.*

Priya Parker describes the importance of a definite and well-done party ending in her incredible book *The Art of Gathering*. She says:

"In so many gatherings, somewhere during the inevitable wind-down, there comes a moment when the host or the guests or some combination make a faint, usually futile bid to prolong it. We often take these bids to be charming, and sometimes indeed they are. But they are also symptoms of gatherings that lack a clear closing."

The book continues:

"Accepting the impermanence of a gathering is part of the art. When we vaguely try to extend our gatherings, we are not only living in denial, we are also depriving our gathering of the kind of closing that gives it the chance of enduring in people's hearts."

 PARTY PRO TIP

If your party is still going strong when it is time to end, give your guests the name and address of a nearby restaurant or bar. Suggest they go there to continue their conversations.

It may seem counterintuitive to kick everyone out when they are still having fun. But when you do, your guests will respect your hosting skills. You conclude your event with plenty of time to tidy, recover, and recharge. And your guests will leave wanting more and looking forward to your next party.

Telling Everyone It Is Almost Time to Leave

Ten minutes before your party is scheduled to end, give your guests notice that you plan to end the party soon. Make a last call for alcohol. I turn down the music, sound my party harmonica, and then say this:

> What a great group tonight. I am so happy with how things turned out. It brings me great joy to see so many of my friends talking together. But the time now is 8:50. I said that this party would go until 9:00. I'm going to respect your time because I know it's a school night, and I want you to come back when I host another party. We're

going to finish up soon. There are about ten minutes left if you want to grab one more drink and say your goodbyes. Thank you all for coming.

Then I keep the music turned down and begin tidying my apartment as a cue that it's time to start wrapping up conversations. Regan Starr, the guy who asks people to fix themselves a drink after icebreakers to keep the energy moving, follows a similar tactic when it's time to get people to leave:

> "After you thanked everyone and indicated it's time to leave soon, stay in motion. Do not stand in one spot. If you have extra snacks, give them away. This is a generous way to reinforce it's time to go.

> Here's how it worked at my most recent party after the last icebreaker had finished: People picked up conversations or started talking to someone new. I, too, joined a group to talk. After a few minutes, I felt no one knew how to break the inertia of the party. I worried the evening would end with an awkward silence and someone finally saying, 'Uh, I think we're supposed to get going.' Instead, I made the announcement. Then I started to tidy up and I took dishes to the kitchen. I offered an unopened bag of chips and guacamole for someone to take home. People moved towards the kitchen. The conversations wrapped up, and the evening concluded naturally."

HOW TO BRING YOUR PARTY TO A CLOSE

- Turn down the music and sound your harmonica.
- Tell everyone it is almost time to leave. Encourage them to get one final drink if they'd like and to say their goodbyes.
- Ten minutes later, sound your harmonica again. Announce that "It's a school night, so I have to kick you all out." Thank guests for coming and start to clean up and tidy as people make their exits.
- If guests continue to linger and you want them to leave, be direct but kind. Gently interrupt their conversations. Tell them it is time to go.

The Last Moments Are the Most Memorable

I like to end my parties on a high note. Sometimes I ask all my guests to circle up, put their hands in the middle, and do a cheer as though we're part of a sports team. I used to do a lot of work with museums, so I get people to cheer the word "museum" at the end of the night. Everyone puts their hands in the middle of a circle, and we do a three, two, one countdown then cheer: Mmmmmuseum!

(I've tried to tell my accountant this makes my parties a business expense, but he's skeptical.)

Doing a cheer at the end of your party sounds silly, but it raises the energy in the room significantly and brings everyone together one last time. My guests love it. Consider doing something like a group cheer to end your party with a word that means something special to you. Like computers. Or avocados. Or even parties.

If behaving like you're a summer camp counselor isn't your thing, then do what feels natural. It's fine to just turn off the music, end the party, and kick everyone out on schedule. Ending your party at the right time can be a high note in itself.

Gently Ask Stragglers to Leave

You'll need to be a bit of a sheriff to end your party. Interrupt ongoing conversations and nicely ask your remaining guests to leave.

People will want to talk and catch up with you before they exit. That's great! It means they like and appreciate you. But now is not your time to chat. Be polite and appreciative, thank them for coming, and say something like this:

> It was so great to see you. I need to wrap this party up now so I can tidy up and get my beauty rest. I'd love to catch up later. Can I message you tomorrow so we can keep talking then?

This lets your guest know you appreciate their presence without being rude. If you have to, play the song "Closing Time" and people will finally get the hint to go.

PARTY PRO TIP

Set an alarm or reminder for twenty minutes after the scheduled end of the party. Use this as an excuse to ask people to leave if you get trapped in conversation.

☑ CHAPTER CHECKLIST

- ☐ Make a commitment to yourself that you'll end your party on time. Know that you're doing it for good reasons.

- ☐ Give a ten-minute warning before you plan to end the party.

- ☐ End on a high note. Do a group cheer or thank everyone for coming.

- ☐ When it's time to go, interrupt conversations as needed. Be polite as you ask guests to leave.

CHAPTER 15

The Day After

Great work. You hosted an amazingly fun, well-attended 2-hour cocktail party. You did it!

Congratulate yourself for all that you've accomplished over the past few weeks in planning your party. You should be proud. You just leveled up in a life skill.

A Personal Post-Party Celebration

It is normal to feel exhausted or even burned out the morning after you've hosted a party. I try to avoid scheduling any important meetings or big work tasks on these days. I will frequently walk in the park or get a massage as a way to decompress.

Xandra Robinson-Burns, a writer and personal development leader in Edinburgh, Scotland, uses the day after to host herself a personal post-party celebration:

> "After the guests leave, I'm invigorated but also exhausted. My ambitious side urges me to start planning the next party right away, but I've learned how important it is to take a moment for myself first. I celebrate the party's success and soak up the satisfied feeling of connecting with all the awesome people I've brought together. This personal post-party celebration helps me to not burn out. By savoring the benefits of hosting, I replenish my motivation and stay in momentum."

Your Own Reflections

Take time to think about your party while it's still fresh on your mind. Some hosts even do this the same night after their last guest leaves. Think about where you succeeded and what benefits you received. Reflect on all the new things that you tried.

- What were your favorite parts of the party?

- What went well?

- What elements of the planning process were most helpful?

- Which beverages and snacks were most and least popular?[1]

- Do you want to host again?

- What do you want to improve upon?

- Who else would you invite next time?

Send a Thank You Message

Send a short message to your guests via email (BCC) or using your event platform. Thank them for coming. Include the group photo that you took.

Subject: Party pic + thank you

Good morning! Thank you for coming last night. Our group photo is attached.

---

[1] I started to make a note of these and immediately found it helpful. For the longest time, I bought cranberry juice for every party and kept throwing it out because nobody drank it.

> Getting everyone together like that really made
> me happy. Can I invite you to the next one?

I keep this message extremely short. I don't want my follow-up message to feel like work. I ask if I can invite them to the next party. This gives an easy way for someone to reply.

Don't feel bad if your guests don't write back to your Thank You message. They're probably just busy. Or perhaps they are bragging to their colleagues about the great party you hosted and all the people they met!

Send me a picture and notes from your party too. It would make me happy to hear from you. My email address is nick@party.pro.

Set a Date for Your Next Party

You'll see the biggest benefits when you host parties frequently. Host every six to eight weeks to keep momentum and develop your relationships. Some people use their positive momentum to set the date for their next party right away. Others prefer to wait a few weeks before going back into party planning mode.

If You're Ready Now

OK, party professional! Choose a date at least four weeks ahead. This gives you plenty of time to start the party planning process again. Come back to this book three weeks before your party date. Review it as you prepare for your next event. If you forgot any steps last time, apply them now.

If You're Not Ready Yet

"Hold your horses, Nick. I've still got my name tag on from last night." Fair enough. Relax in your post-party glory. Recharge your batteries. You've earned it. But at least set a reminder today for when you'll pick your next party date. Perhaps you need a week or two before you can even consider doing it again. Mark a day in your calendar, and commit to picking your next party on that day.

Then get your name tags ready and host that party.

☑ CHAPTER CHECKLIST

☐ Feel proud of what you accomplished. Enjoy a personal post-party celebration.

☐ Reflect on how the party went, including your favorite moments and things you learned.

☐ When you're ready, pick a date for your next party.

☐ Three weeks before your next party, come back to this book.

☐ Great work! You're bringing people together and building new relationships.

Conclusion

Recently, I attended a party in New York's famous Carnegie Hall. It was filled with business owners, vice presidents, and other interesting supporters of the arts—exactly the type of people I like to meet.

When I arrived, I didn't know a single person there. The lights were dimmed. It was loud, and the other guests were dressed extravagantly. The live band didn't show any signs of slowing down. Nobody was even wearing name tags.

Had I been at that party a few years earlier, I would have struggled. Back then, I was unconfident, socially anxious, and inexperienced with the art of party conversation. I looked miserable and uncomfortable at parties because I *was*, so no one wanted to approach me. I would have stuck by the bar, nervously taking too many sips of my water, hoping someone would approach me. I probably would have left too early and spent the rest of the week kicking myself for blowing such an amazing social opportunity.

But this time I was ready.

Because of what I learned while hosting my own parties, I was able to approach new people at the event. I introduced myself and made interesting small talk. I felt confident, and it showed in my body language as I moved around the room engaging with various people, politely excusing myself when I wanted to move on. It was easy for me to smile and laugh. I think people found me approachable and welcoming because I looked like I was having fun—and I was!

I had a great time making new friends at the party. I even led some icebreakers to bring different little groups together and jumpstart conversations with those around me. By the time I left, I had connected with a handful of people both personally and professionally. I invited them all to my next cocktail party.

A few years before, this never would have happened. These days it happens all the time. I'm comfortable not only at my parties but at any event. Now, I always have my next party on the calendar, and my relationships continue to grow.

Look, meeting new people is tough.

"Networking" still sounds like a scam.

I get it.

But damn. Now I love meeting new people. I've found huge rewards in building relationships while hosting my 2-hour cocktail parties.

This is the main reason why I wrote this book—I want others to get the same benefits I got. That includes better connections, more friends, greater social confidence, and new career opportunities. I wrote down everything I learned in order to pass it on.

Your Next Steps

The first party you host is always the hardest, but it will also be an inflection point. It gets easier too.

The value you add to others by creating new connections will come back to you in many different ways. Your professional and social life will flourish. You'll gain new friends, colleagues, and work opportunities. People will invite you to cool stuff. You'll get recognized in town. You'll develop your own personal style. Maybe you'll even find it fun.

This is the end of my guidance, but it's only the beginning of your hosting journey.

You saved a date in your calendar for your first party, right? Have you messaged your core group yet? If not, do those things now. It's a perfect time to follow the formula. Open your email, text messages, and DMs to see who you have recently messaged. That will give you an idea of who might be in your core group.

Once you've hosted a few parties and you're ready to level up your hosting skills, send me an email. I've created a few additional resources. Learn how I send the perfect group message the day after my party. It doubles or triples the new connections that my guests make. Or join me and a few other party hosts in a private forum that I host and moderate. Some of them have applied *The 2-Hour Cocktail Party* to picnics, book swaps, taco parties, and more. Email me at nick@party.pro for links to those.

Hosting small parties changed my life. I can't wait to see what it does for you.

Now go throw a party!

P.S. Please invite me.

Acknowledgments

Illustrations by Fru Pinter.

A teary-eyed, I'm-getting-choked-up-now thank you to all of my friends who helped me write this book. Many, many people helped. Some read early drafts and made countless edits. Others directly suggested new sections, sentences, and even wrote major passages.

Thanks to Nir Iyal, Michael Alexis, Margaret Aiken, Caroline Raasch Alquist, Ashraf Ansari, Jo Banister, Hugh Barker, Daniel Di Bartolo, Jesse Beyroutey, Jarrett Brown, Ben Casnocha, Alan Cassinelli, Victoria Cherry, Grace Clarke, Alisa Cohn, Courtney Confare, Laura Conwill, Niki Cuccinotto, Jon Debly, Tasia Duske, Andrew Flavin, Avi Flombaum, Josh Friedlander, Michael Galpert, George Ge, Adam Gilbert, David Gray, Emily Gray, Susan Gray, Dustin Growick, Harry Guinness, Amit Gupta, Raul Gutierrez, Jason Hackett, Derek

Halpern, Bud Hennekes, David Kadavy, Noah Kagan, Steve Kamb, Anoop Kansupada, Allyson Kapin, Zach Klein, Ashley Knipe, Peter Knox, Brian Kurtzman, Jamie Lafrenier, Richard Lawrence, Gillian Leonard, Dirk Liedig, Bryan Victor Lim, Mo Lima, Freia Lobo, Bethany Mangle, Len Markidan, Rachel McEvoy, Julie Anne Meaney, Neville Medhora, Nate Medina, Arikia Millikan, Neelesh Mittal, Gillian Morris, Wayne Mulligan, Nick Notas, Linda Parker, Tam Pham, Brian Quinn, David Reedy, James Robilotta, Liz Schwarzbach, Ramit Sethi, Anastasia Shcherbakova, Nina Simon, Mike Smith, Regan Starr, Sasha Stern, Carly Straughan, Tammy Swales, Jordan Teshima, Carleen Thio, Jesse Thomas and the JESS3 team, Tynan, Nima Veiseh, Zach Ware, Jonathan Wegener, Aaron Winter, Andria Yu, Natalia Yurevich, and more.

I've posted a full list of thanks with links and a few photos at www.party.pro/thanks.

Cheers especially to those VIPs who helped test and refine this book by hosting their own parties: Nagina Sethi Abdullah, Paul Aguilar, Taryn Cahill, Katherine Conaway, Calvin Correli, Tim Courtney, Matylda Czarnecka, Judhajit De, Brian Dean, Christine Walsh Egan, Justin and Jewels Evans, Chris Fowles, Alex Gates, Seth Hanes, Rachel Hsu, Jay Irwin, Patrick Kanaley, Dan Lerman, Jason McCullough, Luke Murray, Phillip Van Nostrand, Sean Oliver, Phi Pham, Xandra Robinson-Burns, Christina Salerno, Danielle Schulz, Rahul

Shankar, Gena Stanley, Tyler Vawser, Maartje Vos-Swinkels, Rui Zhang, Crystal Zurn, and more.

Thank you to my team at Scribe Media: Brannan Sirratt, Emily Gindlesparger, Mark Chait, Rob Wolf Petersen, Libby Allen, and more.

Thank you to my neighbors who never once called the police with noise complaints.

Appendices

Appendices

EXECUTIVE SUMMARY

To host your own 2-hour cocktail party, follow these basic tips:

- Decide you're going to host a party and commit to it.

- Pick a date for your party three weeks from now, ideally on a Monday, Tuesday, or Wednesday night.

- Keep the length of your party to two hours.

- Invite your friends, colleagues, and neighbors.

- Ask everyone to RSVP and confirm their attendance.

- Space out three reminder messages with fun, relevant information.

At the party, do these four things:

1. Use name tags with first names only.

2. Facilitate three quick icebreakers.

3. Take a group photo.

4. End the party on time.

Follow those guidelines, and you'll have a gathering better than most.

COUNTDOWN CALENDAR

Congratulations! You're hosting your first party. Use this cheat sheet along the way.

The Days Before Your Party

Twenty-One Days Before Your Party

- Set the date and time. Avoid heavyweight days.

- Invite your core group. Send each person a short, personal invite.

Twenty Days Before Your Party

- When you get five yes confirmations from your core group: your party is cleared for takeoff! Make an event page for it on a digital platform such as one listed at www.party.pro/platforms.

- Use the guidelines from Chapter 7 to help write your event description.

- Test sending a link to the event you just made to yourself. RSVP to confirm it works.

- Now reply back to each yes person in your core group. Send them the link. Ask them to RSVP. If they don't RSVP in a day or two, ask again.

Nineteen to Eleven Days Before Your Party

- Start inviting your great guests. Send them a message with basic information about your party. Ask if they are interested or available.

- If they reply with a yes or maybe, send them a link to the event page for more information and to RSVP. If they reply and say no, ask if you can invite them to your next party.

- Collect fifteen total yes RSVPs for your party. If you think you can't get this many, reference Chapter 5 for ideas on how to grow your guest list.

Ten Days Before Your Party

- Purchase supplies, including name tags, cups, a cheap harmonica, markers, alcohol, mixers, and snacks. Reference Chapter 10 for what to buy, or download a printable shopping list at www.party.pro/print.

- Start writing guest bios for your core group. You'll need them for your second reminder message coming up in a few days.

Seven Days Before Your Party

- Send your first reminder message. Use email (put everyone on BCC) or your event platform. Keep it short and fun. Include the date, time, address, link to the RSVP page, and a fun attachment or image.

- For this and future reminders, send it to everyone who has said yes or maybe on the RSVP. For this message only, also send it to people you haven't heard back from yet.

- See Chapter 9 for detailed instructions on this and other reminder messages.

Four Days Before Your Party

- Finish writing your guest bios for at least eight people or half of your guest list (whichever is higher).

- Review the supplies checklist again to make sure you have everything. Reread the section "How to Prepare on the Day of the Party" in Chapter 10 to build your confidence about what's coming up.

Three Days Before Your Party

- Send your second reminder message. Include the guest bios plus the most important party information (date, time, address).

One Day Before Your Party

- Download and print the pre-party checklist from www.party. pro/print or bookmark the section "How to Prepare on the Day of the Party" in Chapter 10 for easy access.

- Review Chapter 12 on beginner icebreakers, and practice how you'll do them. If you're feeling ambitious, reread Chapter 13, and plan to do an advanced icebreaker plus some of the bonus techniques.

- Set out the nonperishable party supplies. Chill your drinks.

- Tomorrow is going to be great. You've put the work in to bring people together and have a great party.

The Day of Your Party

Ten Hours Before

- Send your third and final reminder message. Use the reminder you sent three days before your party as a template. Edit the subject line and introduction.

Two Hours Before

- Prepare your space for the party. Take action on the section "How to Prepare on the Day of the Party" in Chapter 10. Complete the checklist you printed from www.party.pro/print.

Party Start Time

- Welcome your guests with much cheer, especially the first who arrive.

- Delegate duties to early arrivals. Ask someone to help you with drinks and another person to help guests with their bags or coats.

- When four or five guests have arrived, start your first icebreaker. Ask everyone to say their name, what they do for work, and what one of their favorite things to eat for breakfast is.

Forty Minutes After Start

- Turn down the music and do your second icebreaker. Repeat the same one that you did earlier, but now with everyone at the party. Ask everyone to say their name, what they do for work, and what one of their favorite things to eat for breakfast is.

- Keep the icebreaker moving quickly to inject energy into your party. Answers should be thirty seconds or less. Make sure everyone is standing. Don't let people interrupt or ask follow-up questions.

- After the last person, thank everyone, turn the music up, and let new conversations form during unstructured time.

Eighty Minutes After Start

- Gather your group. Take a quick photo. Then run the last and final icebreaker. Use an advanced icebreaker question. Ask everyone to go around the circle and say their name, what they do for work, and what one of their favorite recent pieces of media was (a book they read, TV show or movie, podcast, etc.).

110 Minutes After Start

- Make a last call for alcohol. Tell everyone the party will be ending soon.

120 Minutes After Start

- End your party.

SHOPPING LIST FOR YOUR FIRST PARTY

Available to print as a PDF at www.party.pro/print.

Alcohol

- 750 mL bottles of both whiskey and vodka, or other liquor (tequila!)

- Two bottles each of red and white wine

Mixers

- 4 L of sparkling water or twenty-four cans

- 1 L of cranberry or orange juice

- 1 L each of diet and regular soda

Snacks

- Baby carrots: 1 lb. (450 g)

- Hummus: 8 or 12 oz. (300 g)

- Guacamole: 1 lb. (450 g)

- Chips: two 12–15 oz. bags (370 g)

- Nuts, salted: 16 oz. (450 g)

- Cheese plate: 2 lbs. (900 g) (optional)

- Grapes: 2 lbs. (900 g)

Supplies

- Thirty name tags and four black Sharpie markers

- Disposable cups

- 5 lbs. of ice

- Paper towels or other cleaning supplies for drink spills

- Lightly scented candle for bathroom

HOW TO PREPARE ON THE DAY OF THE PARTY

Available to print as a PDF at www.party.pro/print.

Bathroom(s)

- Remove large bath towels.

- Remove any special medicine or personal items from medicine cabinet.

- Make trash can easily available, empty it, and put fresh bag or liner inside.

- Confirm hand towels or napkins available to dry hands.

- Confirm scented candle. Light the candle.

- Toilet paper roll is full, and extra roll is out. Hand soap ready.

Kitchen

- Clean refrigerator: make space, remove anything old.

- Remove any ice, party drinks, and snacks from refrigerator. Set out.

- Empty trash can. Replace bag or liner.

- Put a sticky note near trash can to clearly label it as *"Trash"* (and recycling).

- Set out paper towels or cleaning stuff for drink/snack spills.

- Wipe down surfaces.

Food and Drinks

- Pour any snacks like chips, nuts, or veggies into bowls or plates.

- Set ice, cups, and marker(s) at bar area. Write your name on your cup.

- Set out water at bar area, or clearly label where guests can find.

Other

- Start playing your party music.

- Set out name tags and markers. Write and put on your name tag.

- Plan where and when you will take your group selfie.

- Make a handwritten *Welcome* sign. Post it outside your door.

EXACTLY WHAT TO SAY

This is a list of all the scripts included in the book.

Pre-Invitation

Event Title Suggestions

- Cocktails and Icebreakers

- Cocktails and Icebreakers with St. Louis's Best

- Cocktails and Icebreakers to Celebrate Spring

Event Description

I'm hosting a cocktail party!

Super casual, meet new friends, see old ones, and have a drink on me.

I'll have name tags, a few bottles of wine, whiskey, vodka, and tons of sparkling water. There'll be chips or light snacks but no formal dinner.

My apartment is on the top floor of a very old building in Greenwich Village. Shoes off inside, please.

It makes me happy to introduce great people and new friends. My favorite part of the night is when we do icebreakers. Have you ever been at a party and wished you could have met even more new, fun, interesting people? Name tags and icebreakers make it easy to do that. Hope to see you soon!

Invitations

Core Group

Hey Derek, I'm thinking of hosting a little cocktail party on Wednesday the 8th at 7 p.m. If I do it, would you come? Can I send you some more info?

Core Group: More Formal

Hi Sandra. I'm planning to host a cocktail party on Wednesday the 8th at 7 p.m. Are you available then? May I send you some more information about it?

Hi Geoff. I want to bring some of my friends and colleagues together for a little cocktail party at my home. I'm looking at Wednesday the 8th at 7 p.m. Are you available then? May I send you some more info?

Core Group: Vulnerable

Hi Casey. I'm reading a book about how to bring my friends together and host a cocktail party. I want to throw my first one on Wednesday the 8th at 7 p.m. Would you come? Can I send you some more info?

Rachel, I want to bring some of my favorite people together and am learning how to host a cocktail party. I am inviting friends and work colleagues to my first one. If I have it on Wednesday the 8th at 7 p.m., would you come? May I send you some more information?

Trying Another Date

Hi again, I'm trying a new date for my cocktail party. Would Tuesday, June 14th at 7 p.m. work?

Core Group RSVP Request

This will be fun. Here is the event info page I just made. Will you do me a favor and click to RSVP? [EVENT LINK HERE]

Full Chat of Core Group Invite and RSVP Request

Me: Hey Derek, I'm thinking of hosting a little cocktail party on Wednesday the 8th at 7 p.m. If I do it, could you come? Can I send you more info?

Derek: Yes, I'm free then. Send me the info.

Me: Great. I'll make an RSVP page and send you more info soon.

[I brew a pot of tea and make the event page.]

Me: This will be fun. Here is the event info

page that I just made. Will you do me a favor and click to RSVP? [EVENT LINK HERE]

Reminder to RSVP

Small reminder: Would you please RSVP here real quick? Only takes a minute and helps me with getting a head count [EVENT LINK HERE]

Great Guest

Hi Mark,

I'm getting some friends and colleagues together for a little cocktail party. Do you want to come?

It'll be on Wednesday, June 8th from 7 to 9 p.m.

I'm hosting it at my apartment at 1000 5th Avenue, NY NY 10028.

I'd love to introduce you to a few people I think you'd hit it off with. I will have name tags and icebreakers because I'm trying to be a good host, haha.

Are you free then? Or can I send you some more info?

—Nick

Great Guest: Informal

Cesar! I'm hosting a little cocktail party on Wed, June 8, from 7 to 9p with name tags and icebreakers (haha). Would love to introduce you to a few friends and colleagues. Are you free then? Or can I send you more info?

Great Guest: Vulnerable

Hi Nina, I'm reading a book on how to host cocktail parties and bring people together. Some friends and work colleagues are coming to my first one on Wednesday the 8th at 7 p.m.

Great Guest: Vulnerable, Book Excuse

Hey Wayne, I'm learning how to host a fun cocktail party as part of a challenge. I'm a bit nervous to do my first one and could really use a friendly face there! Haha. My first one is on Wednesday the 8th at 7p.m.

Great Guest: Yes Reply

Super. This'll be fun. Here's the info page:
[EVENT LINK HERE]
Will you do me a favor and RSVP there so I can get a head count?

Great Guest: *Follow Up if No Response*

Hi again! No reply needed if you're busy, but I wanted to make sure you saw this. Can I send you the party link for more info? It is going to be fun.

Other Messages

Answering Someone's Request on What to Bring

Thank you so much for offering. It is totally not necessary to bring anything. But if you're feeling inspired: a bottle of something you'd like to drink would be great.

Asking Someone to Bring a Friend

I'd like to ask a favor: Will you help me out and bring a friend or colleague to my party? You can send them this message: "My friend Nick is hosting a cocktail party on Wednesday the 8th at 7 p.m. It will be fun! May I share your info with him to send you the information?"

Denying Someone's Request to Bring a Guest

I wish I could let you bring them! But my party is already full with the maximum number that I'm comfortable hosting. Part of the purpose of this party is for me to practice being a better host. More people makes it harder to manage. Is that OK?

Reminders

Please see Chapter 9 for more details about the nuances of each of these.

Seven Days Before

Subject: Party next week

Hey everyone, ONE WEEK AWAY!

The party is next week on Wednesday, June 8, 2022, from 7-9 p.m. It is shaping up to be lots of fun. Looking forward to seeing you.

As a reminder, here is the page you RSVP'd on: [EVENT LINK HERE]

Three Days Before

Subject: Party info ⚡ for Wednesday

Look at this great group of people!

A few friends who are coming to my Cocktails and Icebreakers party are listed below.

Date: Wednesday, June 8, 2022
Time: 7:00-9:00 p.m.
Location: my apartment at
1000 5th Avenue, NY NY 10028
** shoes off inside, so wear nice socks if you want

More info: the event page where you RSVP'd is here [EVENT LINK HERE]

My phone number is +1-212-555-5555 -- Nick

✎ **Guest bios for Wednesday night**
Rob Simon works as a copywriter. He rides a scooter and recently rescued a dog…
[additional guest bios here]
…plus a few more great people!

One of the reasons I'm hosting this party is to introduce my friends and colleagues. (The other is to have an excuse to wear my new red socks.) Perhaps these fun facts will inspire you to strike up a new conversation.

See you soon

—Nick

P.S. Congrats on getting to the end of this very long email 😄

Morning of the Party

Subject: Party TONIGHT! ☆

Wow. Great people are coming.
I've got some liquor, wine, and lots of seltzer.
Plus a few salty snacks.
I'm pretty sure that's all we need 😁

EXACTLY WHAT TO SAY

Time: 7:00–9:00 p.m.

Location: my apartment at
1000 5th Avenue, NY NY 10028
** buzz #5 outside, then buzz #5 again
** shoes off inside, so wear nice socks if you
want

More info: the event page where you RSVP'd is
here [EVENT LINK HERE]

My phone number is +1-212-555-5555 -- Nick

✎ **Guest bios for tonight**

Rob Simon lives in Bali and works as a writer.
He rides a scooter and recently rescued a dog...
[additional guest bios here]
...plus a few more fun folks.

See you tonight!

—Nick

Morning of the Party, More Formal

Subject: Cocktail party tonight

I am excited for tonight. We have such a great
group of people attending. Looking forward to
introducing everyone and seeing you all soon.
I've got drinks, name tags, and icebreakers
ready.

Invitation continues as prior example, including time, address, my contact information, and guest bios.

At the Party

How to Welcome an Early Guest

Laura! Welcome! Oh wow, you are the first person to arrive. I am so glad you are here and that you're here first. Tonight is going to be a lot of fun.

Delegating Bar Duties

Laura, since you're here now, can you please help me with something? It would be a big help if you stand by the bar area and get drinks for the first few others who arrive.

First Icebreaker

All right everybody. What a great group of friends! Let's come over here to circle up and stand together. You all showed up early or right on time. Thank you for that. You're great.

I want us to go around the circle and do a quick icebreaker so we can get a survey of who's here. Say your name, what you do for work, and what one your favorite things to eat for breakfast is. If you don't want to talk about work, you can say something you're passionate about instead—like a hobby or charity.

Then look to the person to your left or right and check whether it's OK that you move to them next by saying, "I'll go first, and then can I go to you?" If they agree, say again:

> Great. So, I'll go first, and then I'll go to you, and we'll go around the circle in that same direction.

Conclusion After the Last Person Closes the Icebreaker

> Thank you. Great job everyone. We just did this icebreaker and there are great people here and more coming soon. Go make yourself a drink, say hi to someone new, and we'll do another icebreaker in about twenty minutes.

Second Icebreaker

Use the same scripts as the first icebreaker.

Third Icebreaker, Five-Minute Warning

> Hey everyone! Good evening! It makes me so happy to see everyone having conversations. In about five minutes, we're going to do our last and final icebreaker of the night. I'm going to tell you the question in case you need a minute to prepare or think about it. The question will be: What's a great piece of media you consumed recently, and what did you like about it? It could be a podcast, a movie, an article, a great book, a fun reality TV show, whatever. Something that made you think or that you want to share. I'll sound my harmonica again in a few minutes to circle up, and we'll also do a group photo then. For now, grab another drink or freshen up. I'll be back in a few minutes.

Third Icebreaker

We're going to go around the circle again for this last round of icebreakers. Say your name, tell us again what you do for work or something you're passionate about, and then tell us about a great piece of media that you've consumed recently and what you liked about it. It could be in the last month or however long. That could be a movie, book, magazine article, TV show, etc. Something fun or that made you think or that you want to share. I'll go first...

Why We Do Icebreakers

I'm so happy to have you all here. The reason I like to do these icebreakers is that I want you all to meet and talk to more people at my party. Maybe you'll hear something neat that inspires you to strike up a new conversation.

Ending the Party

Ten-Minute Warning

What a great group tonight. I am so happy with how things turned out. It brings me great joy to see so many of my friends talking together. But the time now is 8:50. I said that this party would go until 9:00. I'm going to respect your time because I know it's a school night, and I want you to come back when I host another party. We're going to finish up soon. There are about ten minutes left if you want to grab one more drink and say your goodbyes. Thank you all for coming.

Time to Go

It was so great to see you. I need to wrap this party up now so I can tidy up and get my beauty rest. I'd love to catch up later. Can I message you tomorrow so we can keep talking then?

Author's Notes

Formal

Trends in hosting can change over time. Certain suggestions may need to be updated. For corrections and updates, visit www.party.pro/updates.

More Casual

Hi and holy cow. Nick here. I am so dang happy that you read all the way to the end. If this book has helped you, it really helps me if you leave a review on Amazon or Goodreads. I read every review posted there, so I'm sure to see it.

I might update certain elements of my party formula. Maybe there's a hot new platform for collecting RSVPs, a cultural shift that could help you make more connections, or a global pandemic that makes hosting indoors unsafe. Take a quick look now at www.party.pro/updates to see if I've listed any updates or corrections.

Finally, if you want to get in touch, my email is nick@party.pro and add me as @NickGrayNews on most social media platforms. Say hi!

About the Author

Nick Gray moved to New York City with very few friends and less-than-stellar social skills. But Nick craved new relationships and exciting opportunities. He started hosting non-traditional parties—a move that opened doors he never could have imagined.

Today, after hosting hundreds of 2-hour parties, he counts business owners, artists, and inspiring teachers among a circle of friends that helped him launch a multimillion-dollar company. Featured in *The New York Times* and *The Wall Street Journal*, Nick has been called a host of "culturally significant parties" by *New York Magazine*.

More at www.NickGray.net or @NickGrayNews on all the socials.

Made in United States
North Haven, CT
29 April 2023

36027970R00153